# SANAT KUMARA

Dictations through the Messenger
Tatyana Nicholaevna Mickushina
(from 2005 through 2015)

UDC 141.339=111=03.161.1
BBC 87.7+86.4
    M59

M59 Mickushina, T.N.

# Sanat Kumara.

**Masters of Wisdom.** – T.N. Mickushina. –
– 2016. – 250 c. – (Series "Masters of Wisdom").

This book continues the Masters of Wisdom series of books.

This series of books presents collections of Messages from different Masters who are most well-known to modern humanity. These Messages were transmitted through the Messenger Tatyana N. Mickushina, who has been working under the guidance of the Masters of Wisdom since 2004. Using a special method, T. N. Mickushina has received Messages from over 50 Beings of Light.

This book contains selected Messages from Sanat Kumara, a Great Divine Being. Many Teachings are given in the Messages, including the Teachings about the following:

• True and false messengers

• Communities of the Holy Spirit

• Responsibility for the fulfillment of the duties which one has taken on before incarnation

• Proper use of the money energy

• One's choice between the Eternal world and the temporary world

• Overcoming the ego

• The Path of Initiations and much more

ISBN-13:978-1530555734
ISBN-10:1530555736

# Contents

4

# Instead of Preface

## You must be imbued with a sense of reverence about a great sacrifice that Sanat Kumara made for your life-streams

**Zarathustra**
**December 27, 2012**

I AM Zarathustra!

I have come again!

Today we will consider one more facet of the Divine Truth.

At the time of my embodiment I was a prophet of a religion that is not known very well on the Earth now. However, at that time it was on the cutting edge of the religions of the age. And if we make a comparison with the currently existing religious systems, then to some extent I was well in advance of my age, as well as of all currently existing systems of religious outlook. It was I who gave an understanding about the foundation of human nature as of fire and flame. And I affirmed the

7

cult of fire and the cult of a fiery solar Deity from whom humanity had been granted the capability to reason. I affirmed the cult of Ahura Mazda. This great individuality is known in the history of humankind by many names. Now you know this individuality as Sanat Kumara.

Yes, I was the prophet of Sanat Kumara. I still worship His greatness, the greatness of this High Spirit.

Thanks to this Spirit the entire humanity of the Earth was able to continue their evolution. And it is too unjust to forget the great deed of the Spirit of this high individuality. It is too dishonorable to consign to oblivion that Being to whom humanity still owes its continuing evolution.

I must tell you this story. The story that some of you probably heard many times, but others of you might read this story for the first time.

From time immemorial, the situation on the planet started to worsen. And no one man could keep and maintain his Divine nature anymore. Even the lowest chakras could not sustain the vibrations of the Spirit anymore.

All humanity completely blocked its access to the Divine energy.

It was many millions of years ago, and the situation on the planet then was a good deal like the situation on the planet in your time.

There was nobody on the whole planet who could sustain the Flame of Life, the Divine fire in his chakras.

There was not any being on the planet who could transmit the Divine energy into the world.

According to the Law, a world that had withdrawn itself from God was liable for destruction due to its being an unsuccessful civilization.

God had already planned a new lila[1] for planet Earth.

However, a very high individuality was found who vouched for the planet and for its evolutions.

And literally in the last moment the decision was made that the evolutions of planet Earth were to continue their existence but only if there was at least one man in embodiment on the Earth who could sustain the level of the Divine consciousness.

The first who assumed the cross of incarnation on the dark planet was Sanat Kumara. He sacrificed all of His attainments in order to come into incarnation and to give the Divine principles of government and understanding of the Divine Law to the evolutions of planet Earth.

Thanks to this great deed of Spirit millions of life-streams were able to continue the evolution on planet Earth.

I must note that some time ago, all of you were incarnated on the planet in that dark time. All of you are obliged to Sanat Kumara for continuing your evolution now.

---

[1] Lila is a concept within Hinduism meaning "pastime," "sport," or "play" (Translator's footnote).

How many of you remember that? How many of you keep their gratitude to Lord Sanat Kumara in their hearts?

Millions of years passed since then. Sanat Kumara has come to the planet again and again in order to sustain the necessary level of consciousness. And I am proud of the fact that I had the honor of being His prophet.

Sanat Kumara, Ahura Mazda, gave an understanding of the Law through me as His prophet.

A long time has elapsed since then. But in each of the founders of all the religions of the world that appeared here and there on the globe since then, this great individuality — Sanat Kumara — was always present. There were other great souls who were present in either one or another prophet or founder of religions, but at least for a while Sanat Kumara was present in every authentic prophet. The inner guidance that was received by the incarnated messenger of the Heavens has allowed the transmission of the Divine guidelines and the Law of this Universe for humanity in each of the epochs, here and there on the globe.

For the fact that human evolution continues, humanity is obliged to the Great Spirit — Sanat Kumara.

I use this opportunity to come to you and give this Teaching. For I know that this Messenger will apply all the efforts and will do even the impossible so that this Message of mine is left and recorded for you and your descendants.

The Knowledge of the Ancient Teaching, its fundamentals, must be constantly present on the globe either in the form of sacred texts or in the auras of our messengers and prophets.

It is a great Grace for the world that Sanat Kumara is continuing His service for the benefit of the evolutions of planet Earth.

And now, when you know who you are obliged to for the continuation of your evolution, you will not be capable of irresponsible spending of your Divine energy. For millions of years Sanat Kumara has been crucified on the cross of matter so that your souls could strengthen and assume responsibility upon themselves for the planet and for their own evolution.

You cannot pretend any longer that you know nothing. You must manifest all your consciousness and be imbued with a sense of reverence before the great sacrifice that Sanat Kumara made for your life-streams.

I have come today in order to reveal your ancient history for you so that you can more consciously and with gratitude treat that great Grace of the Heavens that has been granted to humanity of the Earth for millions of years.

Each of your acts of sending Love and gratitude to Sanat Kumara and all the prophets and messengers of the past and present who taught humanity the Great Divine Truth will be considered by the Karmic Board as a sign that humanity shows the level of consciousness which is enough in order to be granted new mercies and dispensations.

I have come, and now I leave you.

Try not to forget this Message of mine in the bustle and chaos reigning in your world.

Great responsibility lies with you together with the transmission of this Message of mine.

Do guard yourselves and the Divine flames inside of you!

**I AM Zarathustra!**

Whenever doubts overtake you, and the fog of illusion thickens, keep my image in front of you.

I am putting my presence on this image, and each time that you look at it in difficult moments of your life, I will be able to provide you with effective assistance through this image.

In your world it is just my image; in my world, on the other side of my image, it is my hand stretched out to you, and holding it you can get out of a difficult life situation or a bad state of consciousness.

**Sanat Kumara**
**December 20, 2007**

I AM Sanat Kumara, who has come to you again on this day. I have come with the goal to get across the Divine Truth to you.

You dreamt about gaining access to the fullness of the Divine Truth in your hearts. Now the time is coming when the Word of God should be open to you — not because this Word has been incomprehensible to you until now, but because your hearts have been closed to the Divine Truth.

**Sanat Kumara**
**July 18, 2006**

# Time has changed

## March 4, 2005

I AM Sanat Kumara, and I have come today to inform the world about a new opportunity and a new dispensation which the Heavens have decided to free through our new Russian Messenger Tatyana.

This turn of events will be unexpected for many of you. Many of you will experience contradictory feelings while reading this message.

However, we do not want to force anybody to believe or not to believe the things to be told. Our task is to give you this knowledge. Its acceptance is a matter of your own free will.

Times have changed and the New Age has come. The worlds have converged. Things that seemed to be an impossible dream a few years ago, even last year, are starting to become real now. We are getting an opportunity to speak through many of you and we are using this opportunity.

The situation on earth continues to be stressed. The level of the planet's vibrations is rising. New energies are coming to earth. Due to these energies the majority of mankind feels that it is impossible and senseless to follow further those paths which people have been following for many thousands of years.

This is manifested as a feeling of dissatisfaction, heart sadness, and expectation of something that may happen at any moment. The most sensitive people have lost interest in their usual activities. It seems to them that the things which were important and made up their life before are absolutely meaningless today. All your previous activities — your way of wasting time with friends, watching endless serials, your race for new trivialities — seem to have lost their sense. All this resembles festive tinsel left in place after yesterday's party. Nowadays it is deprived of any sense.

The most sensitive people have a presentiment of the New World and of everything new that is coming to take the place of the old and obsolete. Human consciousness will try to clutch at its habitual precepts, at the religious, social, and family traditions of old. All of these will be wiped off the face of the earth by the wind of the changes to come. There is not much point in resisting these changes because everything in this world is bending to Divine cycles. And the free will is, in fact, limited by temporal and spatial frameworks.

The human mortal consciousness, limited by the framework of the material world, suggests that everything in this world should be subordinate to the will of Man or to the will of human leaders.

No! There is a time to scatter stones and a time to gather them.

If a cancerous tumor makes its home in a human body, a healthy organism starts to free itself of bad cells. Exactly the same principle works in this universe.

If any human civilization concentrates only on the satisfying of personal interests and thinks only about enjoying this world, such a civilization is to be annihilated, just as a cancerous tumor can be removed by a surgeon.

Any resistance is useless in this case. Everything not capable of assimilating New Consciousness, the principles of the Common Weal, Goodness, Cooperation, and God's Guidance, will be wiped off the face of the earth just as the recent earthquake and tsunami killed several hundreds of thousands of people in a few hours.

Stop focusing only on getting pleasure in this world. There are much greater pleasures available to those who open their hearts and minds to the vibrations of the Higher Planes.

There are no things necessary for you outside of yourself. All Divine Knowledge and perfection is inside of you. Seek this treasure in your hearts; seek the entrance to countless riches inside of you.

But you will have to pay for this entrance, and the price for that is your ego. You have to leave your temporal part to get rid of all the accumulations of your electronic belt that are tying you down to earth and the lower plane of this planet like ropes.

Thus, the state of melancholy experienced by many of you now is a sure sign of both your tiredness of this world's pleasures and of your readiness to make contact with the higher planes.

All you need is simply to make a choice and to step into boundlessness, having given up yesterday's festive tinsel. You should take a step towards the reality; one step, then a second one, and continue moving without a stop towards the very true Being which is your authentic essence.

There is nothing outside of you that keeps you from moving towards the higher reality. It is you, and only you, who prevents yourself from doing so.

Can't you cope with your own double wandering in this unreal world for thousands and thousands of embodiments?

You have no other Path. You must either take a step toward the everlasting reality or be no more as individuals. A healthy organism can get rid of cancerous cells by itself. Metaphorically speaking, all of you are in God's belly. Do you really think God will let you live in your own fashion? I say "No." He will simply free himself of everything not matching His Will and His Law.

Think over the words I have told you. I am looking forward to meeting you in the future through this messenger or through any other person who prepares his temple to let me be his guest.

**I AM Sanat Kumara. Om.**

# We show you the Path

## March 15, 2005

I AM Sanat Kumara. I have come. It has become a tradition to give dictations through this messenger. We will continue doing this until internal or external conditions change.

Due to the present state of the world, it is a great rarity to obtain a pure enough transmitter for the perception of our information.

In the course of the reading of these dictations you have met with doubts in your consciousness. Actually, there is a certain difference between the information presented by us and its final version received in the course of transmitting it through the people-messengers embodied now.

But this difference is connected with a greater degree of freedom. We try to give information not only in the framework of the old Teachings — received by people during previous years — but to broaden your understanding of the higher world as well. Any system of world outlook, regardless of its well-knit argument, describes the higher reality roughly enough. Therefore, we have chosen another way of giving information without becoming attached to any existing system of terminology. As you may notice, we use almost no terms which were used before in other religious and philosophical systems.

Our intention is simple: the Truth must be set forth in such an accessible way that even a child can understand it.

You can notice at times that different systems are notable for their complexity. Yes, the organization of the universe is very sophisticated and is hardly comprehensible for human consciousness at the present stage of its development.

Therefore, regardless of our attempts to set forth some things in a simple way, you are not capable of perceiving them. So we have chosen another way. This is the way of giving you and your knowledge a correct direction. When you realize which direction is to be chosen for your movement, you will be able to provide for every eventuality on your path. You will find instruments of the Spirit suitable for you and spiritual practices and methodologies as well. But you will no longer wander here and there because your inner orienteer and the compass of your consciousness will have a correct direction.

The process of giving this direction is very delicate so as not to cause its rejection from your external consciousness. Have you noticed that all, or almost all, of the information transmitted by us through this messenger is acceptable for you? Your critical mind seeks things to cling to, while your consciousness seeks contradictions; and it does not find them.

That is because the higher the level at which the Truth is stated, the more difficult it is to find contradictions.

We can give such an example. You see a peak in front of you: the Peak of Divine Consciousness covered by a shining snow-white cap. But when you set off to this Peak, you enter a woods, wander along the clefts, climb the cliffs, and no longer see the Peak in front of you.

This can be compared to your entering the structure of any church or organization with its regulations, settings, dogmas, etc. You are literally ensnared by impassable bushes of dogmas and rules. Nobody remembers any longer what these rules were made for. But you are demanded to follow them by any means; otherwise you will either burn in hell or all the imaginable disasters of this world will happen to you.

But if you remember — constantly remember — the Peak of Divine Consciousness that you are aspiring to, you will pass through these bushes with thorns that clutch at you, and they will not harm you.

Exactly so, when you enter a thick forest of dogmas from centuries-old religions and do not see even the blue sky behind these dogmas and regulations, you recollect the Divine Peak that you are going to, and you find the way out.

When you continue your way and start climbing the cliffs and stone clefts of new teachings — the new-sprung and thus very slippery and unstable ones —

you recollect the Divine Peak. And you get help and support which can be a hand of a friend or a just rope thrown to you by the brothers who have already ascended higher.

These dictations are not for those who have found rest on a forest glade near a stream surrounded by twittering birds and fluttering butterflies. Such glades are like those teachings and sects where you are told to strive for bliss while dwelling in your world, to love everybody, and to manifest only good human qualities.

There cannot be real perfection in your world. The longer you play saints, the more painful is the blow you must undergo. This blow will awaken you from lethargy on your beautiful glade and will inspire you to climb the peak, overcoming yourselves and your imperfection. As you climb, all your old sores and injuries received in this and previous incarnations will reveal themselves.

But you will continue to move forward, surmounting pains from these injuries, contusions, wounds, and cuts.

Our task is to give you the Path, the right direction. But you will go by yourselves, each by your own individual path.

But after having acquired a correct direction, you will never lose your path again.

We show you the Path to the highest peak of comprehension of the Divine Reality.

Here is the Path. Do go. Do aspire. Only do not stop in your evolution.

Forward!

**I AM Sanat Kumara, and I AM with you along the whole length of your Path.**

# The Earth is living through a critical time at present

## March 22, 2005

I AM Sanat Kumara. I have come through my messenger again.

A verbal explanation of the forthcoming events can reflect only a small part of these events and has a very approximate and probabilistic character.

At the very moment when the entire creation was started all the future events were already planned in the form of their probability.

In our world there are such notions as the zodiac and the signs of the zodiac. For a person acquainted with the language of stars, all the present and future events are already written down in the information field formed by the manifested stars. If you could master the language of stars perfectly, then you would be able to read the future of your planet written in the universal language of this universe.

But you can hardly find a temporal astrologist capable of understanding this language at present.

The true knowledge that is the key to the language of stars and allows us to foresee the future is hidden from contemporary man, just in the same way that you are not permitted to foresee death and know your future and past. This knowledge is also hidden from you.

But the future and the past are determined by the present, by every minute and every second of your present. Time and space limits are actual for your world. There are no such limits in the Higher Worlds. That is why the perfect matrix of creation can manifest itself in space-temporal coordinates in many ways, but the probability of these ways is determined by your every-minute choice.

Therefore, the plan for the universe's evolution, which also includes the plan for your planet, can change within a definite range, but this range is limited by frames. If the evolution of some planet takes place somewhere on the boundary of the channel set up for this planet by the Highest Plan, the whole Hierarchy of Space Beings interferes to correct this evolution when necessary.

It has happened many times with your planet already. The evolution would reach some certain critical point and turn back to the former safe channel.

The danger for evolution appears when it cuts itself off from the Higher Forces and the Hierarchs of the universe, from God and the Divine Law.

There are certain critical points in the history of any planet as well as in the history of the Earth. These critical points are determined by the zodiac and its cosmic cycles. At these points we check whether the information field of the Space Law and its direction are in conformity with the direction of the evolution of the life-streams on the planet. At these moments, the evolution of the planet is corrected when the deflection of the evolution from the direction originally set up exceeds the critical point.

Nowadays, a similar phenomenon takes place. The evolution of the planet has deflected from the trajectory set up by the Space Law, and it requires a correction.

We come recurrently through different prophets and messengers to remind you about the governing Law and the necessity to observe it.

All the predictions of the past and present about the doomsday and different disasters are nothing else but reminders for you about the necessity to obey the Law governing this universe.

The Law will be observed independently of whether you wish to obey it or not.

The Higher Forces have always taken aim to hold mankind on the edge of the precipice and to restrain it from self-destruction.

We have always helped mankind and we help it now to broaden the consciousness of people, to help them overcome their inner limitations, and to ascend to the next level of the evolution of consciousness.

The Earth is living through a critical time at present. The task that lies before mankind now is to realize the fact that apart from the physical plane there are also higher planes and that Man is a Great Space Spiritual Being. Man's potential is great.

But mastering this potential will not happen until Man overcomes those traits that are tying him down to the physical plane.

When we watch some of you from the higher plane where we ascended, we sometimes have the same feelings as you have when watching an ant.

You may have watched an ant dragging a large burden towards its ant hill. From your level you can better see the path it should take. You see that the path could have been shorter, and the ant-hill could have been reached faster and with less force applied.

If you watch an ant, then you will understand the feelings we have when watching your evolution.

In the same way, if you set yourselves to do an ant's job, then we cannot fulfill it for you because your tasks must be performed by you.

We may render certain assistance and we are doing it constantly, but only within the frames permitted by the Law.

One kind of help we give is reminding you of the cosmic deadlines and explaining to you who you are in reality.

Your potential is great. In contradistinction to you, an ant will not be able to achieve a human form of evolution in this manvantara, i.e., this period of the universe's evolution. But you will still be able to manifest your true Divine nature before the end of this manvantara.

That is why we undertake such great efforts to prevent the destruction of the very physical platform, the Earth, which has sheltered you and grants you a safe environment for life and development.

Each cataclysm, each natural calamity is a consequence of your imperfect consciousness. In truth, you reap the fruit of your disobedience, egoism, and obstinacy when you meet face to face with such manifestations of the elements.

The information fields of mankind and of the Earth are very closely linked and interwoven.

That is why any imperfect thought exerts influence upon the entire planet, spreading round the globe and coming into resonance with similar imperfect thoughts and feelings.

In the same way, thoughts appealing to Weal and Good — positive thought-forms and emotions — improve the stability of the whole planet and contribute to the levelling of the axis of the equator.

Billions of space beings are ready to serve tirelessly day and night to let you exist and evolve in peace, to prevent many of the possible catastrophes and cataclysms or to soften their effect.

But your help must also be included in the actions of the Ascended Hosts.

Meditate on Good, Weal, and Love. Keep internal peace and quietness. Each of you should become a fulcrum on Earth, a conductor of Light. This Light will help you equalize the balance of your planet. This Light will help the Earth in ascending to the next level of evolution.

I am happy to watch the achievements that many of you have reached. I am sincerely glad for your successes on your Path.

In accordance with the Space Law, I cannot come and shake hands with each of you. But you can reach my level in your higher bodies. And I will embrace everybody approaching me and shake hands with him.

**I AM Sanat Kumara.**

# I am patiently waiting for each of you to be ready to join the Hierarchy of Light and to be its vanguard exactly at that place where you are right now

**May 7, 2005**

I AM Sanat Kumara, having come to you through my messenger again.

I HAVE come to talk of the ways of development of our movement and of the ways of development of the external part of the organization which is known to you as the Hierarchy of Light or the Great White Brotherhood.

You are aware of the good orderliness of our actions, and you know about the hierarchic character of our structure.

When our chelas turn the conversation toward the democratic principles that should be established in our external organizations, we cannot help smiling.

Oh no; there is a strict subordination of the lowest to the highest. And this principle of subordination is

32

never discussed. You may build up and develop any organization based on democratic principles. But your organization will have nothing to do with our Hierarchy.

Our organizations have always been based on the principle of complete subordination of all their members to the supreme Law of this universe. The Law of this universe implies subordination of those standing at the lower stage of evolution to those at the higher ones.

It may seem to you that this assertion of my exhortation contradicts the earlier teaching given on the service of the highest to the lowest in this universe.

Beloved, this is an imaginary contradiction.

First, you give up your ego of your own free will, take upon yourselves certain duties concerning your service, and only then are you given the necessary help. This help concerns your service but not your expectations of what you are to get for your service. If your mind is distracted by thoughts of acquiring material values or power privileges during your service, you'd better hold a distance from our external organizations.

It is not worth playing with us within your rules. In the course of time all such players understand all the burden of the karma which they create by playing at being messengers and playing at giving service to the Hierarchy and to God.

Those who are sincere and disinterested in their service are helped and supported by us in all of their undertakings and aspirations which correspond to the Will of God.

A person aspiring to receive personal privileges will be placed within severe conditions where he will have to make a final choice whom to serve, whether he intends to serve God or to continue service to his ego.

What you are watching now in the organizations that have proclaimed themselves as our external organizations is the process of separating the grain from the weeds, both inside the organizations and in the hearts of the individuals representing them.

If you wish to make God play within your rules, well, you will be granted a complete illusion that you have managed to do it. You will obtain a full external effect proving to yourself and to the people around you that you have gained many attainments on the path. But there is a great difference between the external attainments and the inner ones. No matter which ranks you appropriate, in what clothes you dress, with what knick-knacks you decorate yourselves, or your places of worshipping the golden calf, this will in no way be reflected in the level of your merits. Meanwhile, true Christ, barefoot and dressed in simple rags, will have his merits hidden from the eyes of an ignoramus but visible to those whose eyes are open and whose ears are ready to hear the Truth.

Try never to seek external and effective con-firmations of the rightness of our teachings. I will tell you more. The level of human consciousness today is such that, in your opinion, the places of concentration of big masses of believers and great riches represent the irrefutable evidence of the rightness of the given religion or belief and of the support given to it by God himself, yet in reality the Divine Truth is least manifested there and the Divine aspect is least present.

Christ discloses himself in a quiet conversation, among few and sincere disciples.

Crowds of people gather either to gaze at the messiah or to crucify him, and for the majority of people it does not matter much whether they gaze at the real messiah, Christ, or at a famous pop star.

It is very sad to watch human individuals subjected to mass consciousness. The consciousness of the majority of people is so remote from the Divine that it is better for you to remain aloof from human mobs.

In my heart I give birth to a plan for the New Age. I see beautiful flowers blossoming in the hearts of our chelas who have reached the level of consciousness of Christ. I see these flowers opening here and there on the planet.

Every such Christ-like being can and must become an initial crystal bud surrounded by more and more new co-workers. And as a result a beautiful crystal will manifest itself in the physical plane, which will become the community of the Holy Spirit, formed by our devotees who have no other aim but to serve God and the Brotherhood.

You may build up your communities on external democratic principles, but let Christ always hold the supremacy in your communities and in your administration.

A new stage of cooperation has come, and Christ-like beings must unite in the physical plane, first within small organizations and groups that will serve as the buds, matrices, and prototypes of the future structure of the society.

You cannot change the consciousness of all the governments of the world and of all the people on Earth. But you can change your own consciousness to such an extent that it will enable you to unite with similar Christ-like ones in the communities of the Holy Spirit.

I tell you that this task is coming to the fore now. Do sow within your heart a plan of an organization, formed not by millions, not by thousands, but by a few Christ-like beings who have submitted all their life to the implementation of the Will of God and to the implementation of the plans of the Hierarchy for the physical octave.

Every such Christ-like being will have an inner contact with the Brotherhood. In your external activities you will be able to be guided by those principles and exhortations that you will be given during meditations and inner communion with us.

Believe me, it is only your ego and the insufficient purity of your four lower bodies, aura, and chakras that prevent you from implementing our plans for the present moment.

You can change your environment in accordance with the Divine pattern. But for this you must change yourselves and tune into the Brotherhood.

Inside of yourself you should have a tuning fork, a true sound, harmonious with your Higher Self and with God within you. Due to this true note you will be able to find coworkers in the physical plane, to comprehend the Divine plan for the current moment, and to start acting, giving the world around you the right example for imitating and following the correct course.

You must start. Do not wait for a command from outside. All the instructions and commands for what you should do and in which way to perform it will come to you from within — from your heart.

You just start acting and believe that all the Ascended Hosts will help you to realize your plans.

We are beginning a new stage of our movement, and it starts exactly where you are now and at that very moment when you pronounce in your hearts:

**"I am ready, Lord. Take me, Lord, take my knowledge, and take my abilities. Make use of me, Lord, to implement Your plans. Here I AM, Lord. I surrender to Your Will and Your Law. There is no longer anything in me that is not from God. There is nothing separating us. We are united."**

You will make mistakes and fall down, but you must go on moving. And the success of your advancement to the Truth will correspond to the purity and sincerity of your motive.

You are lonely only until you feel your unity with God within you, and through this unity you become united with everybody whose vibrations are in keeping with yours.

Yes, beloved, you are few in number, but there are enough of you embodied now to start acting and to create the communities of the Holy Spirit right in the places where you are at this moment.

I am sending out this impulse of integration to you from my heart.

I am patiently waiting for each of you to be ready to join the Hierarchy of Light and to become its vanguard exactly at that place where you are now.

**I AM Sanat Kumara.**

# A Teaching on true and false messengers

## May 11, 2005

I AM Sanat Kumara, having come to you through my messenger again.

I have come again to testify to the fact that you are living at a blessed time. You understand that every time we come to give a dictation we do it with a certain intention. The purpose of my dictation today is to support the impetus of energy exchange which has been obtained between the octaves.

You understand that, apart from bearing the informational and energetic components, these dictations also serve the function of energy exchange between the octaves. Our aim is to obtain a point of Light located between the worlds. Such a point is of unconditional importance for us. With its help we can establish our presence in your world and provide an embodied messenger with an opportunity to reach our octaves. Whatever one person has the strength to do will sooner or later be mastered by everybody.

We expect you to become able to stay in the point between the worlds. Dwelling in the point between the worlds is the state that you should reach either during this embodiment or during one of your future embodiments.

The duties of a messenger do not mean a post demanding respect and worship. The duties and the mantle of a messenger mean only an opportunity to serve more efficiently in the name of God.

The mantle of a messenger allows the space vibrations to change, and we obtain an opportunity to be present and to give our messages at the point where the worlds join each other.

Think over the opportunity for each of you to develop into such a point. In fact, it is just a question of your choice, your wish, and your aspiration.

To deserve the mantle of a messenger you will have to sacrifice much. You will have to give up everything that ties you down to this world. And if some of you wish to choose the path of apostleship, I will gladly teach you either directly in person or through this messenger.

It is time to part with the usual myth inherent in your world that a messenger is an exceptional person. There are certain limitations connected with your karmic past that can block your path to becoming our messenger, but they cannot prevent you from offering your service in a more limited way that can be very close to the service of a messenger.

Today I would like to give you some explanation of the question concerning the subject widely discussed in your world. It is a question of the false apostleship, false teachers, and the false path.

Today I am determined to clear up this question for you definitively. The question of apostleship, like any other question concerning your world, contains the same duality which is inherent in your world.

Therefore, in reality there are messengers who represent the Forces of Light, the Hierarchy of the Light Forces. And there are messengers who say that they represent the Hierarchy of the Light Forces, but at best they represent just themselves, and at worst they have really given themselves up to the disposal of those forces that can be called the forces of the dark. I prefer to call the latter the forces multiplying the illusion; that is, the forces which at a given moment oppose themselves to the Divine plan for the given stage of evolution in this universe.

What is the difference between the true and the false messengers? What should you be guided by when making a choice? This question is a very serious one because your choice of a messenger to follow determines the side on which you will find yourself at the moment of separating the weeds from the wheat. You may make it appear that you do not need to make any choice and give preference to any messenger, and that you trust only God who is present within you and your Christ Self. And this will be a right stand on the condition that you really have a link with God or with your Christ Self inside of you.

Nevertheless, the majority of people do not have such a link, and consequently they have to be more or less guided by the information that comes to them from outside, from the people who declared themselves as our messengers or teachers.

What is the criterion and where is the difference?

A true messenger will never force you to follow or not to follow him. The task of a messenger is just to deliver the information to the physical plane and to help people orientate themselves in the sea of various religious movements and teachings.

A true messenger needs neither your support nor for you to be their followers. You yourself make a decision of your free will whether or not to be guided in life by the information that comes to you through this messenger. Such qualities as disinterestedness and absence of the desire to make a name and become famous are obligatory. The only task that a messenger should carry out and that we welcome is to spread the Teaching as widely as possible by all available means.

If we examine the category of messengers who have devoted themselves to service to the forces opposed to us, here you will see the exact opposite: they strive to be surrounded by followers and disciples and to use the latter in order to multiply power, control, and wealth in the physical world. Since the forces opposed to us do not have their own source of energy (they preferred to be torn off the only source of energy in this universe — the Divine Energy), they need your energy in the shape of your recognition and worship, and your gifts and tithes to support their existence. Such people will use all their influence to prevent you from receiving access to communication with the Forces of Light on your own. But they are not able to teach you such a communication because they do not possess this communication themselves. All they can do is to attach you to their egregore, formed by the energy of their followers who grant their energy to these false messengers and false teachers.

It will not be easy for you to differentiate because everything looks alike on the surface. You hear the right words. You see the correct actions. You can even experience a state of religious ecstasy. But your spiritual advancement is impossible under the guidance of false teachers. At best you will mark time; at worst you can lose all the impetus of your merits.

Beloved, if you have chosen a true teacher and listen to the words coming to you through our messenger, then the result, the fruit, and the consequence of your correct choice will tell you, not in tens of years and not in your next life, but you will already feel an inner change within the next several months.

Yes, there may be trials and you may fall back, and there may be conflicts and disagreement with your ego and with the false part of yourselves. And these disputes, these trials, and this conflict may be rather painful. But you must understand that in the absence of such a conflict, your false part will not be able to leave you and you will not manage to gain victory over it if you constantly pander to your ego and your wishes.

Sometimes it is necessary to make a cut in order to let out the pus, and this can be painful and very unpleasant. But if you do not get rid of the pus in your organism, the inflammatory process can seize the whole organism and bring it to death.

In your dual world it is not always that unpleasant things are harmful and things that provide pleasure are useful.

That is why, beloved, the gift of making distinctions is the quality which you must beg to be granted to you as a mercy in the first place.

I have to touch upon another important moment: A messenger is a human who stands on the peak of a mountain, and all the lightning and hurricanes strike them in the first instance.

Therefore, there are very few people in your world who can hold their ground on the peak of the Divine consciousness. Many people who had passed our tests and deserved their mantles of messengers were not able to hold their consciousness at the proper level and were subsequently deprived of our mantles.

Therefore, beloved, I completely understand your obstacles connected with the duality of your world and sometimes, the impossibility of obtaining a true idea of these or those people, events, or things.

I can assure you that your Higher Self always knows the Truth. That is why you should trust only your Higher Self, but not the external impressions, words, and even deeds performed by these or those people who have declared themselves as our messengers or your teachers.

44

False teachers and false messengers feed on your energy. Everything they can teach you is to cultivate your ego. Unfortunately, a person with a rather big ego is able to distinguish neither our vibrations nor our true messengers. But we know that sooner or later, trials and situations of life will bring him to our messengers. And after all the ordeals that will fall to his lot, he will be grateful to be granted an opportunity just to sit at the feet of a Guru and to listen to the words of the Truth. And his heart, hardened through suffering, will be deceived neither by the appearance of the Guru nor by the fact that the Guru is not recognized by the powers that be.

Beg for the gift of making distinctions, and you will obtain what you ask for.

**I AM Sanat Kumara.**

# Recommendations that I would like to give you

## May 17, 2005

I AM Sanat Kumara, having come to you through my messenger.

I have come to give you a small Teaching on your relationship with God, the Masters, and your Higher Self. While being in the thick of things, in the bustle of the day, you sometimes find it problematic to live in harmony with the Divine and to see — behind this bustle and the scene of the surrounding world — those eternal and immortal things which have always existed but were hidden from your eyes.

That is why it is very important for you to dispose yourself to the Divine. Try to learn to watch the events occurring around you as if through a screen, as though you are at the theatre and the people around you are actors. If you think over the sense of your life, you will see that in fact you have come to this world to play a certain role. Your roles may change during your life. You can even play different roles during one day. But the feeling of being in a play should never leave you because God has created this world as a gigantic stage where you come to play your parts and go through the training at the same time.

If you are able to keep in mind a long drawn-out image of such a stage where you play your parts, you will soon be able to understand that a Producer of all this grandiose show exists and this Producer does not set Himself to make you play according to some script written in advance. No, in the framework of His general idea you have an opportunity to show your own creative work. You may adopt new roles or change the roles you were playing earlier.

But the time will come when you are sick and tired of your own improvisation, and you turn to the Producer directly and enter into a creative relationship with Him. You will try to understand His idea, and the deeper you grasp the plan of the Creator, the more you act according to His plan.

Then you will already be bored with playing the roles you used to play with such pleasure, because the revealed picture of the plan for this universe will fascinate you and capture all your attention. The more you become imbued with this plan, the more significant roles you will play.

Try not to leave the frames of the play in your life. Do not take in everything around you too seriously. Always remember that the illusion around you is passing and has been created to exist only until the moment when your consciousness is able to look behind it and to see the real Divine world and the real life beyond it.

Your inner state determines the life situations that you get into. As long as you take the surrounding illusion for reality, you will not be able to part with this illusion. Remember that all things in this world are drawn to each other by their vibrations. In fact, it is your consciousness that magnetizes the situations that you get into in life. However, it will be very difficult for you to become free from the illusion in your consciousness; at the least, it will demand a certain time. The point is that the energetic records of the situations in which you have not acted in accordance with the Will of God are contained in your lower bodies. These records have been accumulating there during not just one of your embodiments. Therefore, until the moment when these records are transformed in agreement with the Divine standards and the plan of the Creator for your life-stream, you will get into life situations that will give you the best opportunity to work out your negative records or karma.

A simple knowledge of the laws of karma and the Divine Laws for this universe considerably shortens your path on earth. However, the majority of mankind prefers to study a lot of other information and purely human laws. In other words, mankind has become so keen on its play that it does not yet understand that it is merely a play. We come again and again to remind you about the real world, about your mission and your path. But a rare person is able to divert his attention from the illusion and to focus upon our words and our Teaching.

However, we are in no hurry. Mankind still has its reserves of time for evolution. Sooner or later everybody will finish the earthly school — at least those of you who will be capable of undergoing the further training.

If it were not for the change of the cosmic cycles and the necessity to follow them, we would not tire you with the reading of our messages and divert you from your illusion.

Imagine the actors who have begun to feel their feet to such an extent that they continue to act after the performance has already finished. Mankind resembles such actors these days.

In order to learn something you should constantly preserve a childish state of consciousness, a state of being part of a play. But you should not let the illusion capture your consciousness fully even when you are in the thick of things.

Here are the recommendations that I would like to give you.

In agreement with the law of the cosmic cycles, your consciousness is to undergo considerable changes in the near future. And you certainly feel these changes already. It is impossible not to notice them. The vibrations of earth are rising. Those of you whose consciousness is not ready to transit onto a new stage of evolutionary development feel not quite themselves. They try to lower their vibrations artificially, using for this purpose the very means that used to bring the feeling of pleasure to them before. During the period of its existence, mankind has created a whole arsenal of means of blocking its higher abilities completely: alcohol, drugs, tobacco, sex, and games of chance.

But the further use of these means will no longer satisfy you.

The life-giving, Divine, high vibrations, which are gradually coming to earth, will affect mankind more and more strongly, and the lowering of the vibrations will unsettle you more and more from the general vibration in the environment. You will have to give up everything not corresponding to the Divine plan. Of course, the process of the raising of the vibrations has a gradual character. Mankind will not be able to give up its old habits instantaneously. But everybody who feels an inner inducement and a wish to break away from his former habits and old flames will get our help and support.

You will be surprised by the simplicity with which you will manage to part with your old habits.

Write a letter to me or to any of the Masters to whom you feel a special affinity. List all the habits and the objects of affection you wish to get rid of. Ask the angels of protection to deliver this letter to the addressee and burn this letter. From this moment you will have to demonstrate your intention to get rid of your bad habits and affections every day. You may make a copy of your letter to the Masters and read your entreaty every day before your praying ritual.

A few months will pass, and you will be rid of your habits and affections.

Your earnest wish is the only thing necessary for that, beloved. If you are burdened with too many habits, then you may appeal with your entreaty to break first one, then another, until you part with of all of them.

Do not forget that, apart from the bad habits, there are firm states of your consciousness that prevent you from assimilating the Divine vibrations. These can be depression, self-pity, condemnation, envy, and the like. In exactly the same way, you may wish to get rid of these inner energies and barriers preventing your evolution.

Everything can be changed, beloved. And Heaven is ready to render you all the help.

But you should make the first step and show your wish to get rid of your imperfections.

Thus, first you understand that some negative quality or a bad habit is present in you.

Then you show your wish to get rid of this imperfection standing in the way of your evolution.

Further on, you confirm your intention to part with this imperfection during as long of a period of time as is necessary for the transmutation of the energies in your aura that contribute to the manifestation of this imperfection.

I want to wish you success in your work on yourself and on your imperfections.

But please; do not look for many imperfections within yourself; you will only cultivate your imperfections by doing this.

If you constantly focus your attention upon beautiful patterns, nature, music, art, and keep aloof from the imperfect, the substitution of the negative energies will take place naturally without any considerable efforts from you.

**I AM Sanat Kumara.**

# I will be with each of you until all of you return Home

## May 20, 2005

I AM Sanat Kumara, having come through my messenger again. I have come to exhort you, to teach you, and to help you comprehend the Divine reality — another world — that exists simultaneously with your world and differs from it only by its vibrations.

Every moment of your dwelling in your world, you can concurrently be in our world. There exists a part of your being which constantly stays in the Higher worlds. This part of your being has been keeping its link and interaction with the Higher reality during all the period of your embodiments in the physical octave.

The cosmic term approaches, and your Higher part envelops itself in lower bodies and descends into the matter.

In proportion, as the surrounding world becomes denser, the connection between your Higher and lower parts gradually severs and becomes at first hardly distinguishable, until it disappears completely. When the materiality of your world reaches its pinnacle, you lose the link with your Higher part.

Therefore, all the authentic spiritual practices which exist in our world are directed on the restoration of this inner link. When you recollect who you actually are and receive an opportunity to commune with your Higher part, you will become able to change your vibrations in accordance with your wish.

You continue to stay in the physical world, and at the same time your consciousness rises to such a level where at certain moments you become able to get information and knowledge from our world.

At all times, many outstanding figures have been able to raise the rate of their vibrations spontaneously and involuntarily and find themselves in the higher etheric octaves while keeping their consciousness vigil. It is from these octaves that they always extracted inspiration and examples for their works of art, creative works, scientific knowledge, and inventions.

Every discovery has always been made by the people having certain access to our reality.

Nowadays, the capability of the mutual penetration of the worlds and the ability of your consciousness to penetrate into our world will be raised many times.

You will receive your Holy Spirit's gifts and will indeed obtain magic abilities. All this is waiting for you in the near future. The only thing holding you up is your attachment to the physical world and your imperfections.

You should obtain an ability to discern things in you that are not from God and to give them up gradually. At first, you will be able to obtain a commune with us and with your Higher part only on the condition that you lead an absolutely isolated life and avoid any influence of mass culture and people liable to such influence. This resembles pathfinders climbing bare cliffs of the Divine consciousness. For these pathfinders, their efforts and toil are titanic in truth, requiring all their strength and abilities given by God.

Not many people succeed in ascending the summit of the Divine consciousness nowadays. This Path is so heavy that one can fail to hold on to the achieved height and can fall at any moment.

But those who follow the pathfinders will find themselves in a much easier situation. I foresee the appearance of the communities in various places on earth already in the nearest future. Such communities will consist of the people who have obtained a certain level of the Christ consciousness.

These communities will become the prototypes and matrices of the future settlements and the future structure of the human society. While combining industrial duties and spiritual service, such communities will be completely independent and autonomous from the surrounding world.

I foresee the establishment of absolutely new principles of state, temporal power in the places where such communities of the Holy Spirit will form in due course. In the places with the maximum number of such communities, the conditions for the advent of the Golden Age will be created.

I hope that such communities will appear, first of all, in the territory of Russia, for this country by its historical traditions has always been predisposed to carrying on collective management. The complication was in the fact that certain forces have always profited cleverly from this national quality and have manipulated this penchant of the people for communal labor for their mercenary aims.

I also want to draw your attention to the fact that there cannot be an ideal community until every member of the collective fellowship reaches a certain level of individual Christhood and stops using the achievements of the communal labor and creative work for his mercenary and egoistic aims.

Thus, we see that again the same question comes to the foreground before each of you, and this is the question of your personal aspiration to perfect yourselves in God, to give up your ego, and to take care about the purity of your four lower bodies.

I would like to attract your attention to one vital thing. In fact, there are two paths leading to perfecting oneself in God. The first path lies through solitude and prayer, and it is easier. The second path runs through your work on yourself, when you do not need to give up your usual mode of life.

Each of these paths has its advantages and drawbacks. If the only barrier hindering your start of the serious work on yourself is the environment that you are in at a given place on your Path, and you automatically reject any serious self-training because you consider these outer conditions not to be suitable for doing it, then I must remind you that the conditions you are in now correspond to the level of your consciousness and to the correlation between your negative and positive karma. Therefore, the starting conditions will be different for each of you. You will have to overcome all the inconveniences of your outer conditions and karmic circumstances. But you should realize that you deserve the circumstances of your current life because of your own choices in this and previous lives. Lamenting the bad conditions and the disharmonious environment is just a mere excuse for your ego not to do anything. But many people simply fall too low to blame God and the Masters directly for the circumstances of their external life.

Therefore, the first step on your Path is your humility before the circumstances in which you start your Path and your decision to follow the Path leading you back to God, irrespective of any external conditions of your life.

Believe me, if you manifest aspiration and resoluteness in following the Path, you will receive all the necessary ministration. In the course of time the circumstances of your life will change and soften the manifestations of any karmic limitations, even of the heaviest ones. And, in proportion to the changes in your consciousness, you will receive everything necessary for your spiritual unfoldment and perfecting yourself in God.

All the barriers and limitations lie inside of you. All your limitations are just the clogs of the negative energy in your four lower bodies.

Imagine that your four lower bodies represent an attic where all your junk has been dumped during a few thousand years. Meanwhile, this attic has become so cluttered and dusty that now it is impossible even to enter it. The four lower bodies in the majority of people represent exactly such attics.

That is why you should make a decision one fine day to start clearing up the karmic encumbrance of your attic.

Of course, you will not be able to do it in just one day and probably not even in a few years. But the sooner you make your decision and start acting, the faster you will be done with the dirty and tiring job of clearing up your consciousness and sub-consciousness where you have been shoving all your psychological problems with enviable persistence during the entire period of your embodiment on earth.

It is natural that when your problems emerge one after another from your sub-consciousness, you will have to make considerable efforts to overcome these problems and part with them forever. It is like taking old things out of your attic and feeling how they stir in you very painful reminiscences, which give you unbearable pain at times.

Nevertheless, you should be filled with steadfastness and throw away the unnecessary things, and with this become free from a part of the negative energy clogged in you.

In this connection, I would like to warn beforehand all those who look forward to enjoying a pleasant way of spending their time along the whole length of their Path leading Home: Do not expect an easy path; be ready for any unexpectedness. You never know which energy will emerge from your karmic loads. Sometimes your actions will have no logical explanation for them. You will come across people to whom you will feel tempestuous but groundless feelings. Strange things will happen to you, but you should be ready for everything.

You must constantly remember in your consciousness your decision to come back to God and to raise your consciousness to the level of comprehension of the Higher worlds. You should always remember that you are not alone. We vigilantly watch everybody who dares to climb the cliff of the Divine consciousness, and in the last resort we will always give you a hand in a crucial situation. If your motives are pure, you have nothing to be scared of.

The purity of your aspirations shrouds you in an invulnerable defense of the Light.

Each of us passed the same Path during our stay on earth. The Path has been verified. Therefore, do get ready to set out and take a daring step on the Path.

**I AM Sanat Kumara, and I will be with each of you until you all return Home.**

# All that happens is exactly what you admit in your consciousness

**June 15, 2005**

I AM Sanat Kumara. I have come to you.

Each of my comings and each of the comings of the other Beings of Light make your consciousness capable of receiving more and more information. This fact does not depend on whether this information comes to you in the form of words, images, or energy. The very exchange between our worlds is of the essence.

The constant attention you pay to the reading these dictations represents the energy that you give to our world. Your energy flows where your attention is directed. This is a well-known truth. In exactly the same way, the attention we pay to you during the process of giving of these dictations is directed to your world.

I direct the energy of my attention to you. You direct the energy of your attention to me. Thus, we can exchange energies between our octaves. And the more Beings of Light and embodied individuals join this energy exchange, the closer our worlds are.

The process of the energy exchange between our octaves was conceived from the very start of the creation of this universe. But the point of materiality that you have reached at present hinders this exchange. That is why every attempt to restore the exchange between the octaves brings mutual benefit to our worlds.

The worlds are united through the energy exchange. The energies of your world tinted with imperfection cannot penetrate our world. Only those energies that are tinted with Love and bear Good are capable of penetrating the veil.

The majority of people cannot feel the energies we are tirelessly sending to your world because these are very high energies to be sensed. Your sensory organs are not yet capable of perceiving these energies. But the most sensitive individuals can still feel our vibrations even through the distortions that inevitably appear when the energy passes through the veil into your world. No matter how perfect the conductor is, any conductor of our energies distorts them. There is no perfection in your world. And any person, if he approaches our world through his vibrations, cannot stay in your world any longer.

The process of the mutual penetration of our worlds has a very lasting character and can be long-drawn for millions of years.

You are not able to achieve in a moment the level of consciousness inherent in our world. This will be like a burst of a hyper nova for your being.

But we also cannot happen to be in your world — this is like death for us. That is why we have many ways of indirectly penetrating your world with the help of those individuals whose vibrations' frequency allows us to be present within them at least for an insignificant period of time.

You are also able to enter our world. The higher the level of consciousness that you can reach is before your meditation, the higher are the worlds that you can enter.

You are not dense creatures. If you think of yourselves as dense creatures, it can be explained only by the limitation of your consciousness. You rather resemble clouds or bundles of energy capable of penetrating and percolating into our world. When you move consciousness into our world, the latter becomes for you as dense as your physical world.

The whole point is in your consciousness. All that happens is exactly what you admit in your consciousness. That is why you are told about the widening and elevating of your consciousness and about the ascending onto a higher level.

If you could look at your activity on planet Earth with our eyes, you would be astonished by the limitation of your existence. Actually, you are as if in a dungeon within your physical shape. And you cannot get out of your dungeon until an impulse of aspiration to freedom takes hold of you.

I am speaking in general terms and I am giving the hints. It is not because I cannot tell you more — I can tell you much more. But your consciousness is not able to receive the things that it cannot understand yet.

Therefore, the evolution of the human consciousness is measured very well. It is very much like the evolution of the human society. If some decades ago somebody had tried to explain to you how the Internet or cellular phones worked, you would have considered this to be a fantasy and a chimera. So, first we provide an image and transmit it into the heads of the people capable of receiving it. Then this image becomes enhanced with a physical shape and details.

Therefore, we are tirelessly sending our images of the future for this planet through a lot of people.

You receive these images while you are sleeping and waking. The high energies of my native planet Venus have approached. They are elevating the rougher vibrations of your planet by intermixing with them and by gradually transforming the basic dominating vibration characteristic of your planet.

The Earth is very hospitable. A lot of evolutions have found asylum here. The consciousness of some people is ready to transit to a new level and is close to this level or has already transited to it, while the consciousness of other people is not yet awakened at all.

Nevertheless, we have acclaimed the Victory, and the Victory achieved is really great — 144,000 beings embodied on planet Earth have obtained the level of the Christ Consciousness. This means that we will be able to intensify our presence on planet Earth through these beings.

All of these beings are capable of establishing a connection among them on the horizontal level.

All the organizations founded by these beings and all their future projects will bear the high vibrations of our octaves. Consequently, even those individuals whose consciousness are dwelling in a deep lethargy and are not able to feel our energies at present will be able to perceive our energies very soon after having been adapted to their perception through these currently embodied Christ beings.

Two-thousand years ago, Jesus came to earth and gave his Teaching. Just imagine 144,000 beings who have realized their Christ-potential now and how much more they can affect the world and its development.

In fact, every sphere of human activity will come under the influence of these Christ beings, scattered around the globe and involved in different kinds of activity in their professional fields.

It is impossible to measure the process of the transformation of consciousness with physical devices. You just acquire an ability to see more. You see the reasons for the actions, and you see the consequences. You see how it is possible to correct any disharmonious manifestations in the surrounding life. And when you gradually get rid of the extreme negative manifestations in all the spheres of your life, you start to release many souls from the negative influence, first of all the children and the youth.

Soft music and the communication with nature are able to affect the soul of a child much more positively than you can imagine. But when you do not care what music your children listen to and in what company they spend their free time, you cultivate the reasons for your future problems.

Throw away everything unnecessary from your life, the things you can exist without, and you will obtain much free time for your spiritual unfoldment, for communications, and meditations.

The simplest things that you can do in your life, which not only do not require big financial expenses but also release you from many such expenses, are able to bring you to literally revolutionary changes in your life — to the leap in your consciousness.

Revise your traditions and habits and find strength in yourselves to get rid of everything unnecessary that does not contribute to your spiritual development.

This advice is very simple and it will bring you to a definite result very quickly.

You may think and understand what prevents you from following these simple recommendations. The answer to this question is obvious — it is your ego that finds thousands of reasons and thousands of excuses in order not to allow you to change anything in your life.

Now you can see your actual enemy — your only enemy. Your ego, your unreal part, is your actual and only enemy. Therefore, do not seek any enemies around you. Your entire environment just corresponds to you by the level of your vibrations.

The pieces of advice I am giving today are verbatim what I said to the people of earth when I was incarnated on this planet myself. Millions of years have passed. I repeat the same advice for you word for word.

If I were you, I would die of shame. Yet, you go on doing nothing and stroking your ego. Have you ever thought that your experiment with your free will can be brought to a stop?

Have you ever thought that sometimes a gardener has to cut and burn dry branches in order not to give the infection a chance to spread onto the healthy plants?

Has not the time come when this work must be carried out and is being carried out already?

You always have a chance to return to the Path which was predestined for you and which will bring you Home. I ask you to think over my words. Is it too much to sacrifice in order to free yourselves from everything that prevents you from setting forward?

**I AM Sanat Kumara.**

# Use this opportunity given to you by God to go through training and to receive homilies

## June 25, 2005

I AM Sanat Kumara, having come to you through my messenger again. Every time, we lower our vibrations to the physical plane with the help of this physical conductor, and by means of these dictations their level rises.

As we amass experience, we become able to tell more and to transmit more purely, in spite of the fact that the situation around our messenger in the physical and in the higher planes sometimes prevents the transmitting of our message with maximum effect.

This experiment in the message receiving from the etheric octaves has been going on for three and a half months already, and it can be continued provided that we are able to maintain the purity of both the channel and the messenger in the future.

The essence of this experiment is to allow the souls who are ready to perceive the transmitted information to receive our energies continually and daily during a long period of time. The point is that the physical world is like a bog sucking the consciousness of people as if in quicksand. When your feet are floundering into a morass, you do not at first feel any uneasiness. But then a moment comes when the quicksand sucks you under more and more, and you no longer have the strength to get out of it by yourself. That is why we are giving you the rope of these dictations which you can hold on to in order to get out of the swamp of the mass consciousness.

We provide you with an opportunity to receive a portion of the Divine Energy every day while you are receiving and reading these dictations.

In order to learn something even at a normal school or college, you should attend to your studies daily and make efforts to master the material given to you. It is unlikely that you will master all the necessary information if you do not exert efforts daily and do not attend to your studies systematically. The Divine Science training and the receiving of the Divine Knowledge do not differ from any other training and education that you can get in the physical plane.

Therefore, the more systematically you read these dictations, the more effect you will attain in the expansion of your consciousness.

Do not forget that all of you are at different stages of knowing the Divine reality. And for some of you even such a simple presentation of information that we adhere to while giving the dictations seems to be too sophisticated or causes irritation exactly due to its simplicity.

If after finishing high school you find yourself right at the last course of the university, you will scarcely be able to adapt quickly and understand the subjects taught there, even though the information is given in your native language and its presentation is simple enough.

It is not always the case that the seeming simplicity of the presentation means that the information given is simple. The Divine Truth is very simple in its essence, but its perception by the human consciousness does not always take place because the Divine world is distinct in nature and laws from the physical world. And you have to perceive the things that are not perceptible for your physical sense organs. Hence, the difficulties in mastering the material occur together with the doubts and the unwillingness to spend your time learning the subjects that, as you think, are not connected with your life at all.

Actually, there are no instructions in these dictations on how to achieve success in your earthly life, to acquire wealth and to deserve recognition.

There is nothing in these dictations for those people who have chosen the physical plane and the material world as the main focus of their endeavors. These dictations contain no useful information for them, because everything that is stated in the dictations is necessary for the raising of your consciousness to the required level that will enable you to transit to another higher world — the world with higher vibrations.

If you meet a person totally concentrated on the material world and start telling him about the information you get from these dictations, this person will most probably think you are not all there. It is impossible to believe in what you cannot touch with your own hands and see with your own eyes. That is why it is vital for you to refine the perception of the surrounding reality.

When you watch many TV programs or listen to your radio, it can be compared to driving nails with a very sensitive device capable of discriminating microns. Your organism is inherently unique and it enables you to sense higher worlds and to distinguish their vibrations. Therefore, please use your organism for its designed purpose. Protect yourself from any rough and imperfect manifestations of your world. When you start paying too much attention to any imperfect activity, you lower your vibrations and lose the ability to distinguish the things belonging to the higher world, and you no longer notice the manifestations of the higher world in your life. Your state changes during the day, from day to day, and this explains the fact that your heart opens to some dictations while some of them displease you.

The advancement on the Path of knowing the Divine reality has a very measured character. That is why with the help of these dictations we try to maintain your vibrations on a high enough level during as long a time as possible until your consciousness is able to distinguish the rough vibrations of this world and to avoid them from the sense of self-preservation.

Before a ship reaches a safe harbor, it covers thousands of miles on the stormy sea and wild ocean. Only the reminiscences of their own Home and the wish to go ashore force the mariners to ride out the pressure of life's storms.

You need a compass in your voyage, you need a map, you must have skills in reading a compass, in understanding the grid coordinates, and in star fixing in order to reach a safe harbor near your Home. That is why we give you the direction and the instructions and we put you on the right Path. But you should always remember that a moment will come when you can find yourselves alone on the wild ocean. And it will depend only on your abilities and skills acquired during the period of training whether you will be able to overcome the barriers and reach this safe harbor.

Therefore, do not be lazy. Use this opportunity to go through training and to receive homilies granted to you by God. Acquire the skills in compass and map reading, and in celestial orientation on your Path.

Do not allow any external circumstances of your life to wall you off from the Divine reality.

Today I give you this homily, because if you do not use the received knowledge in your life you can be deprived of the opportunity to communicate with the Masters directly. And nobody can tell when such a chance will be granted to you again.

We can spend a huge amount of the Divine Energy on maintaining our channel of communication, but if we see that this Energy is not assimilated by you and is not used in your lives, you will be deprived of the Divine opportunity and the Energy.

You do not water a dead wood in your garden, and neither do we because we prefer not to squander the precious Divine Energy.

I hope you will find a free minute to retire and to ponder over my words in the quiet of your heart.

**I AM Sanat Kumara.**

# The time has come to unite all the Forces of Light on the planet

## October 7, 2005

I AM Sanat Kumara. I have come in order to give a small message especially dedicated to the forthcoming trip of the Messenger to the city of Saint-Petersburg. It seems that since the end of the cycle of the dictations, which we have been giving through Tatyana this year, the changes in the reality around you have been insignificant.

However, let me disagree. Changes in the consciousness of those people who wished to read the dictations have exceeded all our expectations. We only have to regret that our messages have not spread across the physical world to the extent that we intended.

On one hand, we can see the colossal leap in the development of the consciousness of those who have read the dictations and accepted them with all their hearts and souls. And on the other hand, we see a completely disastrous state of those light-bearers who have not received access to these messages and, consequently, have not been able to receive the life-giving draught of our energy which is so necessary at this difficult time.

Therefore, my request is still the same: please apply all the necessary efforts in order for these messages to reach every light-bearer not only in Russia but in the entire world.

It is quite logical that citizens of Saint Petersburg, due to the karmic causes inherent to this city and connected with the events of 1917, must apply all their efforts to spread these messages. That is why the first public speech of the messenger will take place in the city of Saint Petersburg. All the previous speeches, as you know, took place in little groups and in the countryside.

That imposes additional responsibility on the residents of this city, whom the messenger also has a karmic connection with due to her previous incarnations in Russia.

The seeming dissonance between the vibrations of the messages and those vibrations that you are used to and that have been typical for other people should not confuse you. Every time we come we have to use those opportunities and abilities, which that particular conductor of our Word possesses.

I am glad that the impulse and the energy that we have put into the transmission of our messages have not been lost and have been supported by the light-bearers of Russia. Please understand that there is no opportunity for us to perform those miraculous transformations, which have been prepared for Russia on the subtle plane, without your direct help and support. Do agree that there is our part of work and there is your part of work, which you are called upon to accomplish. Our might and the pledge of our success reside only in the union of the Ascended Hosts and non-ascended humanity.

I would also like to draw your attention to your unity on the physical plane.

The time has come to unite all Forces of Light on the planet. Let's begin this process, regardless of your religion or group belonging. There is something much greater than those things that separate you. And that greater thing is your Service to Life, God, and all living beings. Unite on the basis of Love, cooperation, and specific actions on the physical plane that you can perform right now.

Do not pay attention to the things that separate you, whether they are particular points of the Teaching or the words of prayers. Concentrate on those common things that should unite you, like Service to Life and Service to the evolutions of the Earth. And the measure of your achievements has always been and remains the sacrifice that you are able to make for the Good of humanity of the Earth and for the Good of the evolution on planet Earth.

Let's concentrate on your heart again. Come inside your heart and feel your Unity and your desire to Serve. There is nothing that has been or is separating you. The future is born in your consciousness. Now, at this moment I am fixing the focus of Unity in your hearts, in the hearts of all who can hear or read my words. And this focus will allow you to only see the Light in the eyes of those people with whom you perform your actions on the physical plane. What you concentrate your attention on receives the Divine Energy that is coming through you into the physical plane. From now on, you will only see the good in your brothers and sisters on the Path. Always remember that everything in this world is a mirror that reflects your consciousness, and people around you will show that side to you, which you note in them. That way, you will be mutually increasing your momentum of achievements and multiplying your energies aimed at the Common Weal and Good.

Live in Joy and Love, and cast away everything that hinders you from residing in God.

**I AM Sanat Kumara, and I have been with you today.**

# We would like to incline you to fulfill new tasks

## December 12, 2005

I AM Sanat Kumara. I have come in order to open the new cycle of dictations that we wish to give through our messenger.

You know that we have already given the dictations through our messenger this year. And it has been an important condition to spread these dictations widely enough among the people of Russia and all over the world.

We are glad that our condition has been met. Thousands of people, not only from Russia but from all over the world, could become familiar with our dictations and receive from the Ascended Hosts the information so necessary for many at the given stage of the evolutionary development.

We are pleased to state that our efforts and our energy have not been wasted in vain. You have completed your portion of the work, and now we can continue what was planned and give some more information related to the events of this year and the following year, concerning what you should prepare for, what you should care about, and what measures to take.

Therefore, I come again, and I wish to declare that no matter how difficult it may be, we will fulfill the obligations given to the mankind of the Earth and render all necessary and feasible help that mankind needs at the given stage of the evolutionary development.

Every time we will be giving our instructions, we will place a particle of the Divine Energy into our messages. And you will drink and enjoy the nectar of the Divine Energy again. Like last time, we are asking our messenger to ensure the appearance of these dictations on the website the same day they will be given. It will give you an opportunity to be virtually present at the reception of these dictations, no matter where you are on the globe. All you will have to do is turn your computer on and get on the Internet.

For those people who do not have access to a computer, we will give you an opportunity to read these dictations a little later through the printed edition.

Now I would like to get to the main thing that we have again come to you for. It concerns the turn of the year and the beginning of the new yearly cycle. We would like to incline you to fulfill new tasks and new goals that you must set for yourselves and fulfill the next year. Therefore, take the information that will be given to you now and in the following dictations seriously.

First, it is necessary to sum up the results of the past year of 2005. We are doing it with great joy because, despite all the twists, turns, and disasters of this year, we were able to achieve the main goal — the transition of the consciousness of many people to the new, higher level. And that has taken place; it has happened! Therefore, the results of this year are impressive, and these results will impact the physical illusion surrounding you without delay.

You will be able to feel those blissful changes that you deserve from your hard work, your prayer vigils, and your deeds that you carry out on the physical plane.

Now, I should say that you have come to your world in order to act. You have come primarily to carry out specific actions on the physical plane. Therefore, you should begin by taking care of and be concerned about the environment around you. Leave alone everything that happens outside your planet and in other worlds and spaces. Believe me, there are enough Beings of Light in Space who are performing their work at a proper level. I suggest that you concentrate on the needs of your planet, particularly on the needs of those peoples who are around you. Take under control everything that you can take under your control. Strive for the Divine patterns of behavior to be manifested in everything that surrounds you. It concerns not only the cleanliness of your homes and workplaces, but also it concerns the cleanliness of your thoughts and your behavior in everything. You are those people who are making an impact on the whole world. With your help will we be able to change this world. Very few people in relation to the total number of people inhabiting the Earth read these dictations. Though you may not believe me, if only just several thousand people in every nation get access to these dictations, and with the help of these dictations change their consciousness, that will be enough to change the situation in their countries and in all countries on the planet. It is important to have points of Light, the support that we can carry out our actions through. And I must tell you that we have received such support this year.

Fortunately, it applies not only to Russia, but also to many other countries of the world, especially Bulgaria, the Ukraine, and some other countries that have an opportunity to read and understand the Russian text. Therefore, the primary task at this point is the translation of these dictations into other languages of the world and, first of all, into English. Since those hurricanes and disasters that America has gone through this year are a direct consequence of its inability to have kept the focus of Light, we have been forced to move it to Russia. Therefore, the extent to which America will be able to perceive our information that we are giving through the Russian messenger, depends on whether America will be able to keep itself as a civilized and highly-developed country in the near future.

Therefore, I am appealing to everyone who reads these dictations and has an opportunity to translate them into English. It is your turn to serve the world. In your hands are the destiny and lives of millions of people who cannot receive our energy and our information, and that is why their countries are exposed and will be exposed to those terrible natural disasters, which they could not even imagine in their consciousness before. I am also asking those people of America who can overcome a bias and perceive the information being given by us through our Russian messenger: "Cast away all prejudices and dogmas of your consciousness. Trust your hearts. Do everything that is in your power to spread the information that is being given by us, in English-speaking countries."

The time for specific practical actions on the physical plane has come, and you must realize that all you have to do in the nearest future is carry out our plans for the physical octave. Do not search for anyone to be found on the other end of the Earth and guide you. You will receive all the guidance, all the support, and all the necessary energy from the inside. We are giving you the knowledge of the Internal Path for that; the Path that all the devotees of all times were following; the Path that you must follow, as there is no more time left to wait and postpone the realization of our plans for planet Earth. Start doing something specific right where you are now. It may be a small thing, it may be the knowledge that is contained in these dictations that you can give to only several people living in the same town as you, or it may be lectures that you will read at school or at work. Use any opportunity to distribute our information, our energies, and our vibrations into your world.

That is what you must do right now, and that is what your main service next year will be.

Therefore, do not waste time on grand preparation for the forthcoming Christmas and New Year's holidays. The best service that you can render to us will be manifested in your deeds, which you will carry out under our guidance coming from the inside.

Learn to listen to the voice of silence coming from within you and giving you an opportunity to experience all over again the bliss of fatherly love of the Heavens, which the Heavens are tirelessly pouring into your world.

**I AM Sanat Kumara, dwelling in the infinite Love for you.**

# Give your Light, your Love, and your support to the people around you

## April 15, 2006

I AM Sanat Kumara, having come to you again.

When we came more than a year ago to give the dictations through our messenger, that event was not noticed by the majority of humankind. And we didn't try to draw attention to that event. The main and most significant events always happen quietly and without being noticed.

We come to speak with humanity of the Earth, and every visit of ours becomes more and more natural for your consciousness like sunrises and sunsets.

We come, and the situation on planet Earth changes with our coming, as every time more and more individuals can get access to these dictations and enjoy the nectar of the Divine Energy contained in them.

Now I have come to remind you once again of those resolute transformations that should happen. <…>

...I make no secret of the fact that the speed of the change depends on each of you who read these dictations because everything that is connected with your physical world and any changes in your world will happen due to the changing of your consciousness.

As always, I will give you some directions and a short Teaching that will help you in changing your consciousness.

Every time, I come with excitement and I feel a tremble in my heart when I have the opportunity to talk to those of you who are incarnated now.

My children, you do not realize and cannot fully realize the whole responsibility that lies on your shoulders.

Quite recently, before you incarnated, many of you had received a huge training and education in the etheric retreats. The best souls were chosen for incarnation in this difficult time.

Therefore, it is very painful to watch these souls, who have already come into incarnation, allow the illusion to take possession of their consciousness to such an extent that they have not only forgotten why they incarnated but have also forgotten all about God, and they have lost in their hearts not only the Divine models but also the moral landmarks too.

It is painful to realize this, but it is more painful to watch these souls making a transition and coming again to the fine plane. The heart bleeds profusely when you see the suffering of these souls. When the curtain falls from their eyes and the plan for which they came into incarnation and that they have not fulfilled gets revealed before them, then the stress that these souls receive is comparable to the most terrible stress a soul can pass through in incarnation. And this stress lies like a heavy burden upon the soul. A lot of efforts from angels who are called upon to cure the souls between incarnations are necessary in order to prepare such a soul before it is able to incarnate on Earth again.

If you treated one another even with a thousandth of the love and care that your soul receives in the period between incarnations in the etheric octaves of Light, then the world would change unrecognizably after a very short time.

What you have to do is to change your attitude toward the people around you.

If you are an old soul having come into incarnation for the enlightenment of the less developed brothers and sisters, remember your duty and the responsibilities that you accepted before the incarnation. No matter how difficult it is for you, do not think about yourselves; think about those near you who need your care.

Sometimes, a tender look or a good word is enough for the soul again to become full of hope and to gain confidence in the day of tomorrow and the meaning of its life.

Think of all these millions of souls who need your help. Not every soul is capable of understanding the

Teaching that we are giving through our messenger. And not every person is capable of taking the book and start reading it. However, you are able to provide your help and support — not by forcing them to read our Teaching — but simply by being next to them and giving them support with a word, deed, or a look.

Do not be disturbed by the people who will not appreciate your efforts. Simply give your Light, your Love, and your support to the people around you. And do not allow your external consciousness to judge anyone: "Here God has given this person up for lost and he is the top of the ignorance and imperfection."

We have provided this Teaching many times and I am repeating it now. Many souls of Light, before they receive incarnation, burden themselves with such large karmic obligations and assume such huge imperfections that sometimes they are not capable in the conditions that exist now on the Earth to overcome these imperfections and work off the karma they assumed.

Therefore, never allow yourselves to judge. Remember that when you are judging, you decrease your vibrations and become not capable of making right choices and giving correct assessments.

Be above judgments and gossips and do not allow these negative energies to take control of you.

Forgive everyone no matter how unjust it seems what people do to you. The forgiveness, as well as humility and sympathy, do not have any limits.

There cannot be too much of any of the Divine qualities. Your world is in such a need of Divine vibrations and Divine qualities that throughout the day you can pour out your Perfection, Good, and Love, and the world will be grateful to you.

However, this gratitude is not obligatory to manifest on the physical plane. On the contrary, you may encounter complete misunderstanding and even hostility. Every manifestation of Divine vibrations and Divine qualities immediately clashes with the manifestation of the opposite qualities that are trying to deafen the high vibrations and to postpone the moment when there will be no imperfection on the Earth anymore.

It is required from you to manifest Divine qualities, regardless of any reaction on the side of the opposite forces. In no way should you submit to provocation on the side of these forces. You can achieve a lot, but you have to be very firm and brave.

It is in this that the complexity of the given moment consists, and it is this very help that we would like to receive from you.

It is characteristic of the present moment that in the life of every human being there will be situations when s/he will clearly see what forces act through him/her and around him/her. And you will be making the choice consciously within yourselves: which forces you will manifest and where you will direct your energy.

Do not let the temporary mistakes disturb you. Do not castigate yourselves because of them. You have made a mistake, you have realized it, you have taken a decision not to repeat it anymore, and continue further.

Do not allow your consciousness to linger on your mistakes for too long. Do not forget that where your attention is directed, there your energy flows.

The most correct thing would be to live in only the moment in which you are present now. The past and the future should not take too much space in your consciousness.

You are living in the present moment, and in this moment you always joyously meet all life difficulties and failures, and you always keep confidence in your strength, that you can overcome everything and that you will come out victoriously from every situation.

Remember that the biggest victory is that which you achieve over your unreal part, while the outer world is only an illusion that does not require your attention. When you stop feeding the illusion with your attention, it stops existing.

I have given you a very important Teaching. I think that you will use this Teaching in the nearest future and will appreciate its inner power.

**I AM Sanat Kumara. Always with you!**

# We cannot make anybody go, but we call you to take the Path

## April 25, 2006

I AM Sanat Kumara, having come to you again!

I have come this day to remind you once again about your duties, which your souls took upon themselves before incarnation. You may not remember these duties, as the veil is still very dense and your outer consciousness forgets everything you heard and learned between incarnations. However, there is something more in you, and this something is the Higher part of yourselves. This part of you has always remembered and still remembers your destination and your Divine plan.

To awaken the memory of your soul is one of the aims of the given dictations. You recall your destination when you experience minutes of unmotivated yearning and despair. It may seem that everything goes without any apparent troubles in your life, but your souls are worried because the time is passing and they cannot accomplish the duties they took on. Therefore, your major task is to establish a connection with your Higher part and to remember your destination.

When you meet something in your life that reminds you of your duties and your destination you tremble, and this feeling is akin to a gentle feeling of first love. This is a very tender, inviting feeling. You cannot fail to notice this state of yours. You may associate this feeling and direct it towards the person who has given your soul the joyful message, which reminded you about your stay in the etheric octaves. And after you have felt this gentle feeling you will aspire to get this experience of recognition again and again. As this feeling does not relate to your physical plane, this state of yours may confuse you. Oh yes, it can be compared with the feeling of first love. And this really is your first love that you felt before your very birth. Enough number of years will pass and you will understand that this feeling is not connected with a particular person in incarnation. This is a more elevated feeling. This is a feeling of Love to the whole Creation, to the whole Life.

Those of you, who understand what I am talking about, are on the threshold of a new life. Physical life continues to exist around you, and at the same time it is as though you pass to another world which exists simultaneously with yours and yet differs from everything around you. You should make the discernment in your consciousness of this state of yours, the state of being simultaneously among the familiar people and circumstances, but understanding that you are not attached to those people and those circumstances. You continue existing in your world, and at the same time you understand that you are not of this world, for you have passed to another, Higher world in your consciousness.

And you begin to realize that the worlds join inside of you. And thanks to you, the Higher world descends to your physical plane.

At first these sensations are so unusual that they occupy your whole being. You enjoy and at the same time wonder at this state of yours.

However, as you continue to exist in your physical world and still have a physical body, the conditions of your world continue to affect you. And as your vibrations have risen and your sense organs have become capable of perceiving the vibrations of the Higher worlds, some manifestations of the common world and its circumstances strike too painfully your sensitive nature.

You feel the difference between yourself and the people around you. And it hurts you deeply that those closest people to you do not understand you. They hear your words, they see you and the changes you have undergone but their level of consciousness does not allow them to understand and to follow you.

This is a very difficult trial. You lose the connection with the closest people, and you are forced to make a choice. You either stay in your present environment and sacrifice your spiritual development, or continue to follow the Path and sacrifice your relationships with friends and relatives.

Believe me, both things are very hard. And the choice will be different in each individual situation. Only you yourself and your soul know what choice you must make.

If it is a goal of your incarnation to sacrifice yourself and your attainments for the good of the people you love and with whom you are karmically connected, you will make your choice and will stay with your close ones. And if the goal of your incarnation is to help many but the connections with your environment hinder you, you will tear all your ties and — as a bird broken free from the cage — soar up towards the sky, clouds, and mountain peaks.

However, I must warn you that if you do not fulfill your karmic duties and do not pay off all your debts, you will very likely create big karma, taking, it would seem, a light and high path. You cannot set out on a long journey not having taken care of the people you are karmically connected with. And no high goal can be a justification for abandoning those who are around you and who need your help.

Therefore, we try not to give concrete recommendations, for it is impossible to give exhaustive and universal recommendations for all the situations in life. Life is too varied and karma is very tangled.

Sometimes a decision strongly denounced by everybody from the human point of view is the only correct one from the Divine point of view, and the correct decision from all human positions contradicts the Divine Law. The Divine Science is the most complex science of all of those that you encounter in your life. And while you may ignore studying all the others of them and calmly pass by the shelves containing the books devoted to these sciences, all of you must master the Divine Science; the only difference is when each will master it.

The time to master the Divine Science has come for many of you. And you cannot do otherwise; you must take the Path of Initiations because you yourselves planned it prior to your incarnation. The others may calmly stay in the thick of life and continue playing their roles and playing with their toys for yet many incarnations. Their consciousness is not yet ready to part with the physical world and to rise to the mountain summits of the Divine Truth cognition. I can only tell you this: Those of you, who have accepted these dictations that we give through our messenger with all their hearts, and wait for every dictation with anticipation and hope, are most likely ready to take the Path and follow it.

Therefore, check with your hearts the feelings you have from this dictation of mine. We cannot make anybody go, but we call you to take the Path.

**I AM Sanat Kumara, always with you!**

# You are forming the new reality in your consciousness

## July 1, 2006

I AM Sanat Kumara, having come again. As it has already become a tradition, I have come to give a message, opening the new cycle of the dictations that we intended to give for mankind of the Earth. This time, I am glad to tell, we are ready to give our messages in Bulgaria, a country which is no less important than Russia, as it is exactly here we plan the creation of conditions necessary for rapid growth of the consciousness of people who live in this country.

We are glad that we are having an opportunity to speak again, as it is not always possible to realize our plans on the Earth. It is connected with big unpredictability of the situation on the Earth, when all our plans are ruined because of a wrong action by only one person. That is always deplorable. However, we hope that there are still a sufficient number of individuals, being incarnated, who will be able to help us in the realization of our plans and intentions.

I have come to remind you once again of the obligations that you have taken upon yourselves before your incarnation. You have been preparing for your missions for many incarnations, and you have all the necessary skills and knowledge in this incarnation. All that impedes your fulfilling of the taken obligations is your fussy, unruly, human mind. Your carnal mind makes you lose your Path, thinking of thousands of reasons and millions of arguments, while your heart's voice keeps on sending you gentle quiet signals, calling you to the Path, to the top, to the manifestation of the plans of the Brotherhood.

Therefore, think once again about the extent of your attachment to the physical world around you, and how important it is for you to listen to your heart's voice and to leave the fuss of the world in order to implement what is destined for this planet. Your planet should become the planet of the developed consciousness. The vibrations of the Earth should allow those beings, who you now call the Ascended Masters, to come into incarnation. They are the Teachers of humankind; and now many of you are incarnated in order to create the conditions on the Earth necessary for their incarnation. Think about that important task that you are facing. Try to track the moment when your consciousness starts slipping down, gradually refusing Divine models and replacing them with merely human aspirations. Your carnal mind starts activating in you as your consciousness approaches the idea of serving us. It is very dodgy, and it gives you the arguments which your outer consciousness cannot neglect. You leave everything to get that piece of bread to satisfy your physical hunger instead of taking care of your spiritual food and the daily bread that Jesus talked about.[2]

Do not think much about how to support your physical existence. Do think only about how to fulfill your Divine plan. Or is there so little Faith in you that you cannot believe that God will take care of you?

The Teaching remains the same. It is given over and over again, and only the dullness of your consciousness and the inertness of matter have made you listen to the same Teaching for many thousands and millions of years, incarnation by incarnation. You listen but cannot hear because every time you deviate from the guidelines you have accepted, and at the moment of the insight, again you rush in pursuit of useless things of the physical world.

It hurts to observe that. Lack of Faith is the main disease of humankind. Look at animals and birds. God takes care of all living creatures. No one dies of hunger living in the natural conditions. Only when man interferes in the Divine Laws with his imperfect consciousness and tries to create, replacing God with himself, do different disasters and cataclysms occur.

Therefore, we repeat over and over again that your only enemy is hiding in your imperfect consciousness, in your heart that does not let God in.

Now I would like to remind you again that at times all the Ascended Hosts, holding their breath, wait for

---

[2] "Give us this day our daily bread" (Matthew 6:9-13).

your choice, the choice that you may or may not make. And the development of evolution on the Earth depends on your every choice. Believe me; everything you do every day is very important. Consider your everyday actions. Try to analyze how long you have been thinking about God and your Divine purpose during the day. How many of you are really ready to sacrifice something for the wellbeing of the world?

Too many speak about serving and about the work they do for God. However, when the talk turns to doing even one small but concrete thing, there are thousands of reasons and arguments that appear which make the person forget about God, about serving, and rush for the things and pleasures which should not have been in your consciousness since long ago.

I have come to you today, and I am very glad that I can give a talk again on that ancient Teaching because each of you who are reading these lines can wake up at any moment in order to start acting in the new reality.

You are forming the new reality in your consciousness. And as soon as you suddenly realize in surprise how aimlessly the people around you waist their energy, you wake up for the new reality and become those warriors-votaries on whom we can rely. The whole institution of Guru-chela relations is oriented for constantly keeping your consciousness at a decent level. It is very seldom that an earthman can manage without outside assistance, and go through the Path of Initiations on his own. I can tell you that if you are not a partial or full incarnation of an Ascended Master, you will not be able to go through your Path and reach the top of the Divine consciousness on your own without the Teacher's help. Therefore, we send our messengers again and again so you could see the Path and remember your obligations and those plans which you intended to implement before your incarnation. You have assumed those plans yourselves in your higher consciousness. Now you have to try and reach the highest state of your consciousness in order to remember everything that you have planned before your incarnation on the Earth.

There are many of those who read our messages. There are those who start going along the Path of Initiations. But only a few pass the tests and continue going along the Path. It was always like that. We hope very much that your time will be an exception, and we will be able to come to thousands and hundreds of thousands of incarnated people to communicate with them at the level of their outer consciousness and to start doing the job of transformation of planet Earth so rapidly that all the changes will be observed by the generation that is living now.

I need volunteers who would wish to serve the Brotherhood. I am personally ready to come to you and help you on condition that your intentions are supported by concrete conscious actions of transformation of the earthmen's consciousness.

**I AM Sanat Kumara, having been with you today, and I hope for future meetings!**

# A Teaching on the karmic responsibility for your actions in the sphere of translating the texts of the dictations and in the sphere of managing cash funds

## July 9, 2006

I AM Sanat Kumara, having come to you again.

From this day forth until the end of the current cycle of dictations, every day before reading a dictation I want you to invoke the electronic presence of the Master giving the dictation. This seemingly simple technique will enable you to feel our presence and will present quite a new view of many theses of our messages because the presence of the Masters during the reading of the messages will many times magnify the effect you experience while reading them. This is a special dispensation, and it will be active still for some time after the completion of this cycle of dictations. You will be able to judge by your gut sense whether this dispensation is still operating or not.

So, in order to invoke the presence of the Master giving a message, you should pronounce either aloud or to yourself:

**"In the name of I AM THAT I AM, I invoke the electronic presence of...** (insert the name of the Master giving the message)."

Try to use this dispensation beginning from today's dictation. Read this dictation to the end and then reread it after having made a call and you will feel the difference. I recommend that you always make such calls before reading the messages we give through this messenger. The operation of the call will be manifested when possible and necessary.

All the Masters can manifest their electronic presence, and the degree of this presence will be in direct ratio to your ability to perceive our vibrations and to the readiness of your higher bodies to distinguish our vibrations.

You know that sometimes we give our messages at a higher level and sometimes we give them at a slightly lower level. And this is not always predicated upon the quality of conductibility of the bodies of our messenger. It is just because there are different levels of development of consciousness in the individuals embodied now. And different individuals are capable of perceiving different information and different energetic components of the messages.

We thoroughly verify the information given. And when your external consciousness starts analyzing the information, this does not always happen to be useful. It is because any critical perception of information cuts short the flux of energy, and the reading of our messages becomes useless for you. A message as such energizes within you a directivity to the energies of the Masters, and you distinguish our energies at the moment of reading the messages. There are keys that energize your higher conductors, and you become able to perceive not only the informational component of the messages but their energetic component as well. This explains the fact that our messages are impossible to retell. A retelling does not carry in itself the keys hidden within the body of the message. You take in our messages as a text written with the help of symbols of this or that language; however, it is not exactly so. A message carries in itself hidden keys. And when you translate our messages into different languages, these keys can be lost. Everything depends on the internality of the translator. If the translator is attuned to us, the translation in itself carries our vibrations. If not, the translation carries only the informational component. This explains the fact that even though you speak another language, you still receive the energetic component of the messages when listening to the dictations being read by our messenger and not understanding the words. You feel the energies and vibrations of the Masters.

If you read our messages translated into your native language, you can lose this energetic component. Accordingly, I recommend that those who translate our dictations into other languages in the future, before starting the translation, invoke the electronic presence of the Master whose dictation you are going to realize and translate. I also advise you to start the translation in a balanced state after a good meditation or a prayer practice.

Any imperfections you have are imposed on the text of the translation. And if you happen to distort the text of the dictation at the process of the translation, the karmic responsibility for the distortion of the Words of the Masters falls on you. Yet, this karmic responsibility of yours can be neutralized by good karma which you acquire at the moment of translating the dictations into other languages and distributing them. But you should bear in mind that good karma is acquired by you only if your motive is pure and you really do translations in order to spread our Teaching, but not in order to earn money.

The question of interrelation with money is one of considerable nicety and difficulty. In reality, money does not come to you when you perform some work for the Brotherhood. But when doing some work for the Brotherhood you receive opportunities, enabling the energy of money to pay back the energetic consumption you incurred while being involved in the work for the Brotherhood.

Everything in this world is based on energy exchange, and any stagnation of energy leads to the shortage of monetary energy. When you have money you should think about where you should spend it. Any accumulation of monetary energy is not useful and represents a sign of karma of incorrect attitude toward money. Think about how you should dispose of the money you have. And if you spend this money on pleasure, next time you will not receive the payback of the monetary energy.

In contrast, if you spend your store of money on good causes, the flux of monetary energy will be intensified, notwithstanding the fact of how much effort you apply to earn the money. You will get a windfall or somebody will give you money under any pretense. Do manage monetary energy correctly. The more you give disinterestedly, the more you receive.

But you should always remember that you are responsible for how much and to whom you give your money, because in the case that the money you give is not used on good deeds, the karma of the misuse of monetary energy will devolve upon you.

In contrast, if you contribute money for good deeds, then good karma of correct use of your money will give you a chance to dispose of this good karma at your sole discretion. Therein lays the principal of the church tithe. It is, essentially, a very right and exact principle, but only if the church or any other religious organization spends your tithe on good deeds — not on multiplying their own property.

The principle of the reasonable and right use of the Divine Energy is manifested in everything, and monetary energy is in no way different from any other kind of energy. One kind of energy turns smoothly into another kind of energy. And your tithe, if you manage it correctly, provides you with the manifestation of opportunities in the physical plane. These opportunities can pour upon you in the form of a flood of cash, a joyful future for your children, your own health, and the health of your nearest and dearest.

Good karma can also be used for your own personal purpose. For this you are given a chance to write letters to the Karmic Board.[3]

Today I have given you a Teaching on the karmic responsibility for your actions in the sphere of translating the texts of the dictations and in the sphere of managing cash funds.

And this vital Teaching requires an immediate use in your lives.

Now, let me leave you and say goodbye for the moment.

**I AM Sanat Kumara. Om**

---

[3] More information about getting help from the Karmic Board is found in the following Dictations: "Let your consciousness go beyond the limits of your family, your city, and your country and take the whole Earth as your native home," Lord Maitreya, June 5, 2007, and "The extension of comprehension of the Law of Karma," Beloved Kuthumi, July 6, 2006. Dictations are available on the websites http://sirius-eng.net (English version) and http://sirius-ru.net (Russian version).

# We give you the Living Word, the Living Teaching, and expect you to bear our Word and our Teaching into the life through concrete work in the physical plane

**July 18, 2006**

I AM Sanat Kumara, who has come to you again on this day. I have come with the goal to get across the Divine Truth to you. You dreamt about gaining access to the fullness of the Divine Truth in your hearts. Now the time is coming when the Word of God should be open to you — not because this Word has been incomprehensible to you until now, but because your hearts have been closed to the Divine Truth.

You can only hear in your hearts what you are ready for and what you are awaiting. In our turn, we are always ready to give you what you strive for. It is very similar to child upbringing. When the children are growing up, the toys that they used to play with become unexciting, and they turn their gaze toward new toys, which their consciousness has grown up to. Gradually, children become adults and enter the adult life, continuing to play the games that their consciousness is ready for in the adult life. Finally, the moment comes when none of the games of the physical world are able to satisfy a person's consciousness, and that means that this person is ready to transition to a new level of consciousness, into a different world.

In the beginning, the transition into that world goes unnoticeably and faintly visible. That world opens up inside of you. At first you feel that other world — different from your physical world — only a little and then more and more. You come in touch with that world in your sleep, during the moments of your enlightenments in the stillness of your heart. That world gradually begins to grow from your hearts into your physical world. Your physical world begins to change, becomes thinner and acquires the characteristics of the subtle world. That penetration of the worlds begins inside of you, and you are that frontline troop of volunteers who are growing into the New World with their consciousness, bringing the coming of that World for the entire planet closer.

This process is happening. It began a long time ago. Lately, this process has been accelerating more and more. The transition into the New World, to the new level of development, may happen much sooner than it had been planned if the rate of growth of your consciousness increases with the same rapid speed.

Believe me, your consciousness is the greatest restraining factor that is hindering the course of the evolution on your planet. You still resemble students who had been held back in school due to not being able to learn the lessons given to them. We had to use many artificial maneuvers in order to drive your development from the deadlock at which you got stuck. Now the dark Middle Ages of your consciousness are coming to an end. The awakening and the dawn of a new day is coming. I am happy to acknowledge this transition of your consciousness to a new level.

The Heavens are rejoicing that such a great number of individuals have reached the state of awakening of their consciousness!

Do not lower your guard, because the morass of the physical world is able to suck in your consciousness again and bring it to a lower level, typical of an animal-human. Remember and always know that you are Gods, and the next stage of your evolution is to finally become man of reason and God-man.

You differ from us only by the level of your consciousness, and many Ascended Masters are ready to sacrifice a part of their causal bodies in order to assure the growth of your consciousness. Indeed, many of the Ascended Masters sacrifice a lot and come into the incarnation partially by penetrating into the individuals who had given permission in the subtle plane for such a co-inhabitation. It allows you to be able to gain a leap in the level of growth of your consciousness. By acquiring such acceleration, you can have an influence on those who are close to you, your relatives, friends and coworkers. Such a leap of your consciousness cannot be hidden from the eyes of the people who have known you for a long time. They will neither be able to explain to themselves what has happened to you nor why they have lost interest and are no longer striving to associate with you. Yet other people, by feeling the vibrations in you that they have been striving for over a long period of time, will find areas of common interest with you. You will become able to unite at a new level of consciousness and create a new future, residing at this new level of consciousness. You can have an influence on everything that surrounds you. The ability to unite and perform joint work is an undeniable proof that you have stepped up to the new level of your consciousness. You can tell other people about your merits and accomplishments as long as you wish, but if your inner accomplishments do not manifest themselves in the physical world in the form of concrete work and results, then those accomplishments of yours are worth nothing. Most likely, it is astral jokers who played a practical joke on you and told you about your greatness, which you have not yet achieved because your level of consciousness does not allow you to rise higher than the astral plane.

All of your accomplishments must be manifested in the physical plane. Your main accomplishment is the ability to collaborate and fulfill concrete work on the physical plane. You should not construct mythical projects on the subtle plane, but roll up your sleeves and build a senior home, a kindergarten for children, plant an orchard, and help your neighbor. There is a lot of work in your world, and all that work is done by those who have made certain spiritual accomplishments, instead of just thinking that they have accomplished something.

In this way, we will be able to change the world by acting through those who have prepared their temple for our arrival and have expressed their readiness to serve.

The time has changed now. In the past it was necessary to say calls and prayers in order for you to work off your karma; now the time has come to perform concrete work on the physical plane. When you begin your collaboration in order to fulfill the plans of the Masters on the physical plane, your karma is being worked off at a flash-like speed. That is the new dispensation for your time. The working off of the karma will be accelerated for those who take concrete actions on the physical plane directed to fulfilling the plans of the Brotherhood.

Our plans remain unchanged for millions of years. Our plans are to give the Teaching and to follow the Teaching. It is especially good if you apply your efforts in the area of upbringing children and young people. That is because in ten or twenty years your efforts will yield real results when the new generation enters the adult life and builds that life based on the Divine principles.

Today I wanted to draw your attention once again to the necessity of your work on your consciousness and your simultaneous collaborative work with each other on the physical plane. There is no time to wait until you become completely perfect. Your aspirations will yield results much faster if you apply all the acquired knowledge in your daily life as soon as you receive it. Whatever does not get reinforced in practice becomes useless, dead knowledge.

We give you the Living Word, the Living Teaching, and expect you to bring our Word and our Teaching into life through concrete work in the physical plane.

**I AM Sanat Kumara with Hope in you and Faith in you.**

# All efforts of your will are required of you not to take the bait of the energies of the past but to aspire to the new day!

## December 20, 2006

I AM Sanat Kumara, having come again in order to tell some joyous news to you! We commence a new cycle of dictations through our Messenger. And, as always, there is a lot to talk about. This process of our communication and our applied efforts is not in vain. Every time we notice more and more new changes in the consciousness of more and more human individuals that are incarnated in this difficult time.

We come in order to reinforce and anchor our focus of Light, our flame, which we have tirelessly carried and given to mankind for millions of years. And now, as never before, we are happy to state that our efforts are so obviously reflected in the minds of people and in the activity that is taking place in the physical plane. We cannot help being surprised by the miracles that have already been manifested and that will be manifested on planet Earth, both with our help and with your help, and with the help of those people who have decided to devote themselves to serving Life and serving mankind of the Earth. Each of you, our devotees, must be aware of the fact that at this difficult and life-changing time one person only may be missing — the one with whom the circuit of the Divine opportunity becomes complete. So, if you are still in the state of indecision and hesitation, I recommend that you stop paying attention to your minor everyday problems as soon as possible and aspire with all your being to us in order to fulfill those tasks which we affirm in your consciousness and to the fulfillment of those tasks which we are calling you to do.

We are never tired of repeating again and again that we need faithful devotees who, at our first call, are ready to rise and go where their efforts and abilities are needed to fulfill the Divine Plan for the sake of which they have now come into incarnation at this hard time for the planet.

I always remind you of your responsibility and your obligations which you have taken upon yourselves before your incarnation, as every time reading our Messages you experience inner thrill and willingness to fulfill your duty. Yet, some time passes and you forget about your obligations and your aspiration, and you succumb to the fuss of life which swamps you like a mire making you rush along the wrong path, the path of chasing momentary blessings and pleasures to the detriment of what is eternal.

And now I would like to remind you once again that the darkest and the most severe time of the year is approaching. This is the New Year's Eve, the new day's eve. It is exactly before the dawn that the night is as dark as never before. That is why the phantoms of the past, the phantoms of your previous blunders and errors in the form of unbalanced energies, will appear around you and arise from your consciousness. These energies will be dragging you away from the Path. All efforts of your will are required of you not to take the bait of these energies of the past but to aspire to the new day!

It is very difficult for you to believe that the thing which I am telling you about is very vital and urgent for you. Believe me. The festive fuss and buzz must not occupy your attention, but rather the tranquil consideration, in the candlelight, of the things you are to do and of the ways to remove the barriers which prevent you from fulfilling your mission. Do not seek for these barriers outside yourselves. Analyze your previous course of life and try to understand what is there within you that hinders you and impedes your advancement along the Path.

You know the Path. You have been shown the Path. Those of you who have gotten an idea about this Path and have felt an urge to overcome inner barriers and imperfections, will never turn away from this Path of Initiations that we are calling you onto, and that is enough to instantly pull you out of the mire of life and like a high-speed elevator raise you to the top of the Divine consciousness. I am glad that many people have aspired. And I am glad that for many people our Messages are the lighthouse which shows the Path in the dark. I am glad that thousands and dozens of thousands of people have awakened, but our task is to wake up millions of the sleeping souls.

Therefore, we come and tirelessly repeat the Teaching, ancient as the world itself. Many of you begin to recollect your previous incarnations and those feats that you performed for the Good of the whole Life. This is not accidental, because now there are so many souls of light incarnated on the planet that the Heavens have literally become deserted, as each of those over the veil is hoping for you with all heart and soul and is endeavoring to help the birth of the new thinking, the new consciousness, based not on the previous dogmas but on the Knowledge and Wisdom of millenniums. You have forgotten about the Wisdom which you were originally taught in our retreats. Now the time has come to return to Divine Wisdom and leave the labyrinths of the carnal mind. Your carnal mind is trying to persuade you and lead you along the secret passages and subterranean labyrinths of wrong logic. However, your immediate task in the near future is to recollect the only true logic, the logic of the Divine World. It does not matter how different this logic is from everything that you have encountered in your life; you have to accept this logic and study it — not with your external consciousness but with your heart. Only then, when you open your hearts and aspire properly, you will be able to comprehend the Divine Law and Divine Wisdom. Only the one who abandons the earthly logic is able to be imbued with the Divine logic. This is the difficulty of your time, as you have to take us on trust and to aspire to those cliffs, sometimes without any safety equipment. Then, if your faith is steadfast, you receive at your disposal the tools which enable you to surmount your path as efficiently as possible. One fine day you will discover that your consciousness has changed unrecognizably and there is no turning back to the past. The Divine Reason within you will triumph over the logic of the carnal mind. We repeat the things which seem obvious. However, a very small number of human individuals can fully comprehend and perceive our Teaching.

All the Divine is very simple. This simplicity frightens off and is doubtful for those who still search for complicated paths and voluntarily drive into the maze of the teachings that lead nowhere but toward the death of the soul. We do not want to scare you, but warn that the cosmic deadlines have approached, and there is no place for the obsolete in the New World. At the turn of the year you must carry out a thorough revision in your minds, in your consciousness, and willfully leave everything that is not Divine and everything that prevents you from your advancement along the Path. You have some time, yet the time is short.

I have been with you today. I am happy with our new meeting.

**I AM Sanat Kumara. Om.**

# The time for choice

## January 7, 2007

I AM Sanat Kumara, having come to you through my Messenger again. I have come quickly in order to transmit an urgent message to you concerning your planet which is going through a difficult time. Do you hear me?

I AM Sanat Kumara, the one who you know as The Ancient of Days, the one who came to your planet in its darkest hour and has not left it even until the present day.

I AM the one who is the most caring father for you. And, being your father, I have come to give you a message concerning the time you are living through.

All of you are in the state of transition of your consciousness to a higher level. All of you must perform the transition in your consciousness. However, there are those among you who do not wish to follow the evolutionary path of development. You decelerate the process of evolution, and that is why the time that we have warned about is coming for you.

Any changes on the planet are possible only if they are authorized by the supreme guiding and coordinating

116

body of this Universe. And so I have come in order to give you the explanation that has just been received which concerns planet Earth and its evolutions.

At the end of this year, those of you who will not manage to overcome the qualities within themselves that prevent you from your advancement on the Path will be especially and forcefully pushed forward in their development.

Unfortunately, those of you who need to receive this message of mine in the first instance hardly read our Dictations that we transmit through our Messenger. However, in the subtle plane you will receive this warning through the consciousness of those who read our messages.

Our warning has been uttered in your physical world hence, everyone in your physical world is able to and must hear it, no matter if you perceive our words with your external consciousness or not. On the inner plane you will receive our message. And you will face the choice whether to follow the evolution or to continue stroking your ego and having fun in the illusion.

There are those people among you for whom the term of the cosmic opportunity has not come yet. And you still have some time, so you may continue your development. However, there are those who have missed all the given deadlines, for them I am giving this message today.

You know it within yourselves to whom this message refers. You are missing one cosmic opportunity after another. You think that there will be no limit for you to shirk from the path of development which is predestined for you. Well, the time has come for you to be very forcefully pushed forward to make your final decision and choose either your further development or you yourselves give up for lost your further development.

God is very merciful. He just leaves those who do not wish to comply with the Law established in this Universe on their own. Those dead end branches of evolutionary development, which you can see on some islands in the oceans where they continue to sit by the fire and devour their chunk of meat, have also previously made their choice — the choice which you are now facing.

In accordance with the new dispensation, you will make this choice consciously. You will know in your external consciousness the final choice that you will make. And we will leave you alone. Evolution will stop existing for you, and you will roll down the stairs backwards for many millennia.

Already by the end of this life you will be watching the fruits of your own choice.

All of you belong to different stages of evolutionary development.

There are representatives of the third, the fourth, the fifth, and already the sixth Root Races among you. Now the time for choice has come for those who must transit on to the next stage but cannot do it because of their laziness and neglect. I am speaking of those representatives of the fifth Root Race who are not eager to follow the upward stairs and continue living as if nothing is going on in the world, as if the time has not changed and all processes have not accelerated.

It behooves you to look into yourselves before the end of this year to realize how you intend to exist further.

Your time has come not because you have fallen behind in your development. Your intellect is alright but you have fallen behind in the results for the development of your soul. The choices which you make push you farther and farther from the evolutionary path of development and make you slip into the evil path, the path of development of the carnal mind. In this case your intellect does not serve you in the best way. You try to solve sophisticated Divine tasks in the terms of your mind. But Divine solutions come only if you reject the earthly human logic and dedicate your entire self, your whole being, to serving the Supreme Law.

So, I have come today with one piece of news that is not very joyous. In order to equalize the balance of energies in your consciousness, I wish to give another, more joyous piece of information.

For those of you who have chosen the path of evolutionary development and who are following this path despite all difficulties that they face in life, I have brought a piece of news concerning a new opportunity and a new dispensation. The opportunity of an accelerated development of your consciousness is opening up for you. Already by the end of this year many of you will notice how quickly your consciousness will change, and these changes of your consciousness will draw to you the people who are going in the same direction with you. You may recognize each other by the burning flame in your eyes, by the beat of your hearts, or by the wonderful and generous giving of yourselves to serving all Life.

You will be able to unite on the new principles and to arrange life on the basis of the Laws that exist in Heaven.

For you we are preparing the projects of our Communities in the subtle plane. Uniting in the physical plane, you will be able to represent the prototypes of new settlements, new communities and new towns.

I am glad to finish today's message on this joyous note!

Always, in all times, there existed an opportunity of making a choice. Some people chose one path; others preferred another choice.

This is the very process that is described in the Bible as the process of separating the wheat from the chaff.[4]

The time has simply changed, and this process which formerly took many lifetimes, you can now watch within your one current lifetime.

I wish you to make only the right choices in your lives and to follow the evolutionary path of development.

With God's blessing!

**I AM Sanat Kumara.**

---

[4] Matthew 13:25-30, 36-43.

# You must devote your whole life to Service

## December 20, 2007

I AM Sanat Kumara, having come to you again through our messenger.

I have come, and I have tears of joy in my eyes!

You cannot even imagine how Heaven rejoices — not only because we have the opportunity to work through our messenger again, but also because there are a lot of sympathetic hearts who are willing to accept our vibrations and follow our guidance!

You know that not so long ago, a few years ago, we were confused because we did not have an opportunity to work through our messengers and did not have this opportunity to reach out to those individuals who are incarnated and seeking contact with us but cannot find it.

So many people are ready and I give today's message for these many people.

Have you ever noticed how much harder it becomes during these days of December? And it is not that you do not feel well. You justify your malaise by excessive overload at work and at home.

The fact is that the decision has been made on the transfer of the Earth to a new vibrational level, and I have come to tell you that there has been one more step taken in the endless series of steps aiming at the approachment of our worlds.

Once you have read this message of mine, do not rush to share this news with your acquaintances and colleagues. I am telling this personally to each of you. And while reading this message each of you will get for himself the meaning, the vibration, which is given to him personally.

Our worlds have neared, and this has become possible thanks to your efforts, thanks to your Faith and your Love. And I am sure that you will be able to fix yourselves at the level that you have reached by now.

There were other people on whom we pinned our hopes and who gladly and enthusiastically took up the implementation of our affairs. Where are they now? Each of them has made his choice and each of them in accordance with the law of free will has plunged in his development many incarnations back.

Therefore, I have come to you today to remind you that every attainment you have reached in your illusory reality requires continuous efforts to master the achieved success.

You cannot afford to sit back and relax in the company of your former friends, and you cannot afford to rest in your favorite places. You have to continue your hard work if you wish your development to go on rising right to the top of Divine consciousness.

Once you allow yourself to relax a little, you slide down to the foot of the mountain.

This is not news, what I urge you to do. We have always been teaching this noble effort through different teachers. You have to be able to combine leisure and work, and in your hearts you should always be prepared to carry out the tasks of the Hierarchy.

Many are ready, many have achieved great heights in their spiritual advancement, but for some unknown reason, when help is required to perform our affairs, they go away and start dealing with "important matters" as they believe. You do not have more important things to do than to help the Hierarchy, to help the evolutions of planet Earth. Your carnal mind will find thousands of arguments for you at this particular moment when the time comes to do that for which you came into this incarnation. And then, when you have to offer your shoulder and carry the burden on the dangerous and difficult section of the Path, you suddenly rush with enviable vigor in the opposite direction. And any signs and even the words that we send to you through our messenger are not perceived by your consciousness.

You are to develop your feature of Service. You must devote your whole life to Service.

My words seem to be very hard and confusing for those who are not ready to accept them. Therefore, I said at the beginning that I am referring to those who are ready, to my children who I have worked with for many incarnations.

A crucial section of the Path has begun for you. And you will have to apply the maximum effort, all your strength and all your abilities accrued by your previous incarnations.

I come to you again, my beloved, my nestlings from my eagle's nest. I have nurtured you with the wisdom of the ages, and I have given you the Divine Energy of Light to drink. I have the right to ask you for help, and I have the right to count on you at this difficult time.

I hope that you will respond to my appeal — even those of you who have made big and small mistakes, do not persist. Come back under my paternal wing. There are no such misconducts which cannot be corrected by selfless Service and devotion to the Masters.

I hope that today's message will give you cheerfulness and will not make you deal with endless soul-searching or lead you into inharmonious states.

All that was in the past is left in the past. You must think about the present and about what you are to do now and how you can carry out your Service.

Now it is not enough to get together in groups for your prayer vigils. You must provide tangible assistance to many souls who still cannot come to the realization of the Divine Law existing in this Universe. We are concerned about many people who still continue to indulge in the illusion and cannot get out of the web into which they have gotten owing to mass culture or rather the lack of culture prevailing in your society.

Each of you should worry about many of the lost souls. Many cannot even see the glimmer of Light in the environment of their lives, as their karma that they have created themselves is very heavy. Each of you, my people, can give them a particle of the Light in order for these lost souls to see another world and other examples that exist. There is something that is Real and that is worth living for.

Sometimes you lack Love and confidence in the correctness of your chosen Path.

Therefore, whenever doubts overtake you, and the fog of illusion thickens, keep my image in front of you. I am putting my presence on this image,[5] and each time that you look at it in difficult moments of your life, I will be able to provide you with effective assistance through this image. In your world it is just my image; in my world, on the other side of my image, it is my hand stretched out to you, and holding it you can get out of a difficult life situation or a bad state of consciousness.

I have come to you on this day, and now I am leaving you. See you later!

**I AM Sanat Kumara. Om**

---

[5] Image of Sanat Kumara on page 15.

# The answers to some questions you are interested in

**March 13, 2008**

I AM Sanat Kumara, having come through my messenger again. I have come to clarify some points for you regarding the apostleship and the relationships of our messenger with other people and regarding her attitude toward different spiritual and religious leaders of the present and the past.

Each messenger has a certain mission. He or she comes into this world with this mission, and in some cases he or she has been preparing for this mission for many hundreds of years.

And now, when our representative comes into embodiment and starts doing his or her work, various things start happening at the same time regarding how the Teaching being given by us combines with what is given through others. Each messenger knows only his or her mission. The task of the messenger is not to give comments on the statements of other teachings that come into the physical world through other people.

Do understand that your world is the karmic world. This means that the truth and the light are mixed with some misconceptions in your world. Everything is relative in your world, and no one can dare say that one of our representatives of the present or the past has or had the entire fullness of the Divine Truth.

Do understand that the same Truth is given at different times for different groups of people who are in incarnation, and every time its interpretation is slightly different.

If you think that we must give comments on the statements of the teaching which have been given through other people, you are mistaken for the simple reason that you need to live here and now and fulfill the mission for which you have come into embodiment instead of wasting time on endless arguments over who was right or wrong one hundred, two hundred, and more years ago.

You can study and compare the statements of various teachings of the past and present. But the truth is that you are to fulfill your Divine mission, and for this you must maintain the constant inner consonance with the higher worlds.

As soon as you follow the path of gossip and appraisal, you lower your vibrations. You descend from the Divine level to the level of the carnal mind; and you can no longer see and distinguish the Divine Truth because Truth is the state of your consciousness, the degree of your consonance with the higher reality.

I also would like to touch upon the question concerning our Hierarchy and various posts which this or that Master known to you holds in our Hierarchy.

Yes, we have given a certain understanding of how our Hierarchy is organized. However, this understanding has been given for your level of consciousness at a certain stage of development. Do understand and try to realize that our world cannot exactly correspond to your world, and do not try to ascribe to our world the structure that exists in your world.

When trying to understand the structure of our world, never aim to get the full impression about our world. Those people who make their transition are in the caring hands of our assistants. Believe me, they have no thoughts of who of us hold what posts in the Hierarchy. They just revel in the Light emanating from us, and they are happy that they are in the place where they do not feel the lack of Love, attention, and care. They can see each life situation on the Earth in a new way. You learn from your mistakes yourselves.

If the Ascended Masters in all their radiance will be forced to come into embodiment and live in those conditions that exist on Earth now, you will never believe these are the Ascended Masters before you. Therefore, the time for the Ascended Masters to come into embodiment on the Earth has not come yet.

Still, many of us keep our presence in those individuals who have been our disciples for many hundreds and thousands of years.

Therefore, we cannot say that this or that Individuality is fully or even partially present in any person because the presence of the Teacher is a temporary phenomenon, and it is determined by the degree of purity in both the bodies of a disciple and the environment surrounding him.

When it is possible for us, we are present on the Earth and can see the situation through the eyes of our disciples.

All messiahs and messengers had the presence of a higher individuality within themselves. During their missions both the degree of the presence and the individuality itself changed. That is why it is wrongful to speak about the embodiment of this or that Master known to you in the body of this or that person. You can only speak about an admixture of the higher individuality and about the extent of its presence.

The Masters, well known to you, whose names you know and call, actually have sometimes absolutely different names, not the names that you know.

We can speak with you about the structure of our world for a long time, and you will seek to peep through the crack of the veil that separates our worlds, but you will be wasting your time in this case because you should focus on your current tasks and live in accordance with the ethical and moral precepts that we give to you.

I have been a little harsh today, and those of you who have been waiting for a concrete answer to your questions may not derive anything. However, I tried to talk to your Higher self and give those exhortations that will allow you to keep correct guidelines in your life.

**I AM Sanat Kumara. Om.**

# News about the current situation

## June 5, 2008

I AM Sanat Kumara, who has come to you again.

The time has come to compare the compasses of your aspirations. The time has come to summarize what has been done.

We were together with you, observing everything carefully from a distance. Now, we would like to provide our comments and pool the intermediary results. You remember that we began a new stage of our work[6] with the present messenger in January of this year.

You remember that this stage is unusual. This stage is the most important one. I have to reassure you in earnest that never before have we put so much effort in order to achieve what we had planned. Each person who comes in the sphere of our interests and our activity

---

[6] Tatyana Mickushina. Dictation "I have come to inform you about the end of another stage of our work and about the beginning of the next one," Beloved El Morya, January 10, 2008. Dictations are available on the websites http://sirius-eng.net (English version) and http://sirius-ru.net (Russian version).

can feel that everything is very serious. You may not see or feel it with your physical senses, but on the level of the intuition, and with the help of secondary tokens, you understand that you have entered a very serious stage. We have not been able to pass through this stage for the past several centuries. This stage is related to building a model in the physical plane.

This image of Community or a settlement will be different for each stage of human evolution and for the conditions on Earth at each period of time.

Now the time has come to acquire the image of Community at a level of consciousness of a new quality. This is to be done using the human achievements that mankind has at the present moment. This task is very difficult and requires a considerable amount of efforts by the light-bearers who are currently incarnated.

Believe me, sometimes everything depends on just one person, who has come into the incarnation for the sake of completing certain work. He or she knew about it and readily started the work. Yet, some time passed and the initial impulse weakened.

Due to your human nature, you are not able to constantly maintain the highest level of your consciousness. Then, a moment comes, when your cunning mind tells you, "Think about yourself. Why do you spend so much energy on this work? Is it genuine? Is it not yet the time to live for yourself? Life is so short."

Then, that person begins to doubt and misses one opportunity after another. Cosmic deadlines pass, and the task remains unfulfilled. If the fate of only one person were involved, one could just lament and regret what has happened. However, I am talking about the missed opportunity for the entire nation and for several generations of people.

Of course, we have alternative options. We immediately try to use an alternative and call another person to action. However, it is very hard for us to see how one light-bearer after another falls off the Path and how the task which they have incarnated to fulfill falters. We spoke about the karma of betrayal many times. However, when a person betrays, he does not understand it in the majority of cases. It seems to him, or rather, his carnal mind persuades him that nothing terrible will happen if he continues this work at a later time when he is ready. However, if only you realized what major forces are concentrated in a small location in order to complete an important job. It is so difficult for us to observe how tons of the Divine energy are wasted only because of one wrong choice made by you.

It is a pity that your world is so thick that you do not realize many things. We prepare our missions for several hundreds of years. We send our best Sons and Daughters of Light in the incarnation to work for the Common Good of the entire planet. Why do you forget your responsibilities at the most important moment?

I have come to remind you about the important work that you are to complete now.

I have come to remind you that the time of real actions has come.

You can no longer spend time on useless talks. Stop arguing about who is more right and whose understanding of the Divine Truth is more correct.

There are fairly genuine criteria which have been tested by time and that we have used working with the mankind of Earth for centuries. If you do not see a result of collective actions in the physical plane, the results that would confirm the truthfulness of the given Teaching, it means that either the teaching is wrong or the participants have not met the hopes of the Ascended Masters. We tirelessly start our work again and again. Only in extremely rare cases do we manage to complete our building process and obtain the desired result in the physical plane.

We always strive to give you a model in the physical plane that you can use to rebuild your world and your relationships.

In order to help you, we are ready to sacrifice a lot. If there were people among you who would be truly ready to sacrifice an equivalent of one millionth of our efforts which we constantly apply, the world would experience a tremendous change in circumstances that would affect all aspects of life and conditions on the planet.

Therefore, do not seek anyone who would be guilty that our missions of Light fail one after another. Simply ask yourself: "Have I done everything in order to help the Ascended Masters from my unascended state?"

You can help us! You can do what we are unable to do. You can be our hands and feet in the physical plane.

I hope very much that you will find the time to look at your life from the highest state of your consciousness that is possible for you. I hope that you will try to break away from the net of your carnal thoughts and desires in order to find the power within you and fulfill your Divine mission.

We need an outpost in the physical plane!

Many forces stand against us. Many people become conduits of the opposing forces. Very few withstand that.

Only few remain faithful and truthful. Eternal glory awaits them. What awaits you when you quit your service and start chasing the trinkets of your world?

No bitterness of defeat can be compared to how many souls we are losing and how many souls step away from our Path.

**I AM Sanat Kumara, with hope to awaken your souls from the sweet dream of illusion.**

# Reminder about Responsibility

## June 20, 2008

I AM Sanat Kumara, who has come to you again through my messenger. I have come on this day and I am glad to announce that the benevolence of the Karmic Board has allowed me to give you today's message. You know that the Karmic Board is holding a session at this time. You also know that such sessions are held twice a year: during the summer and the winter solstice. You are probably somewhat interested to learn the latest news from this session, are you not?

Well, I have come to report them to you. Today, we have made a decision that transmission of messages through our messenger will continue. We had to see how ready you were to fulfill our plans in the physical plane after the end of the last winter cycle of messages.[7] We carefully observed everything that was taking place. Unfortunately, your attitude towards our plans and goals

---

[7] Referring to the cycle of messages from December 20, 2007 – January 10, 2008. Dictations are available on the websites http://sirius-eng.net (English version) and http://sirius-ru.net (Russian version).

sometimes looks dispiriting. We are ready to collaborate with you, and we give you tasks and recommendations. However, every time, again and again, we face your sluggishness and, sometimes, even direct sabotage of our plans. We carefully select an incarnated person and prepare him or her for a certain mission over the course of many years. Some of you come into incarnation with prepared missions. You take on these missions yourselves. You yourselves strive to incarnate. Some time passes before you find our Teaching in the physical plane and come very close to the fulfillment of the goal for which you have incarnated. At times, you need to make only minor efforts and the task will be fulfilled.

In accordance with the Law, at the same time as you start your work for the Brotherhood, a temptation comes to you from the outside world. You get an alternative version for the course of events. You get an opportunity to make a choice. You need to understand that this happens automatically. That is how the Law works. You are given an opportunity to choose for yourselves whether you demonstrate determination, devotion, and perseverance and stay on the path, showing miracles of dedication, unselfishness, and Service, or you follow the temptation that your world is offering to you, and then you choose a longer, more winding path, which in many cases leads to nowhere.

Therefore, every time when we come, we try to warn you about the imminent danger. It seems natural to your mind to be doing what the majority of people are doing. You are young, full of strength and energy, why not live for yourselves a little bit, and enjoy life?

As soon as such a question quietly enters your head, you immediately begin to lower the level of vibrations that you have achieved. You get on a slippery path that leads into a ravine of sufferings and miseries. You need to understand that you yourselves create the circumstances for this and future lives.

As soon as an opportunity to serve the Brotherhood opens up for you, a temptation leading you away from the Path appears simultaneously. When you give in to the whispers of your carnal mind you lose the level of vibrations. And when your Higher Self, your master in the physical plane — and even we ourselves — comes to tell you about your delusion you do not hear us. You do not want to hear.

When you reach a crossway, your master on the physical plane always sees the situation and tells you about it. Then you choose again whether to follow your master or the whispers of your carnal mind.

We give you crutches and look after you like clingy nannies, but you break away from the caring hands and head out to seek adventures, pleasures, and everything that you wish to obtain from the physical world.

You need to understand that what is good for the majority of mankind (for example, gaining life experience and playing the game of illusion) is a serious violation of the Law for those who have come close to us and to our messenger.

Imagine that you are a little child and you allow yourself to frolic. Your parents and everyone who is older than you look at you calmly and try to mentor you on your path. However, when you grow older and continue to frolic in the same way as little children do, you are not allowed to do that anymore. Imagine a child who took someone else's toy that he liked and brought it home. You mother or father, grandmother or grandfather will certainly tell you that you should not take other children's toys. They will take the toy and give it back to the crying toddler who has lost his favorite toy.

However, when you have reached a mature age and are trying to embezzle somebody else's belongings, the society often punishes you in a very strict way. Therefore, do not find excuses in the fact that other people are enjoying the pleasures of life. You carry a completely different responsibility, including karmic responsibility. That is because you have reached a mature age of sons and daughters of God.

Now, when the construction of the Ashram for our messenger is in its full swing, think about whether you have done everything to help us in our construction. How often in the hassles of your life do you remember that we are fulfilling a project on the land of Russia?

You can imagine that centuries pass while we strive towards but cannot attain our goals. And now, when an opportunity to fulfill our plan has come, you find more important duties: you take a vacation to the sea with your girlfriend, you go backpacking to the mountains, or you spend money on a new car or some other expensive thing.

I am calling you to treat all your actions very carefully. From this moment, I am warning you that your karmic responsibility is doubling.

Our every step in the physical world costs us too much for us to peacefully observe how you waste your time, your money, and your life in pursuit of trifles, gadgets, and pleasures.

I came to you today, and the purpose of my visit was to remind you again about the responsibilities that you had accepted before your incarnation. Very recently, when reading the cycles of our messages, in the first flush of enthusiasm you took on responsibilities, which you forgot as soon as you came across another toy in your world.

**I AM Sanat Kumara, warning you about the responsibility of your actions.**

# About the situation in the world

## October 12, 2008

I AM Sanat Kumara, having come to you today to give some explanations regarding the events taking place in the world. You know from the mass media reports that the financial situation in the world is unfavorable; you know about earthquakes which have become more frequent; you know about hurricanes and typhoons that almost constantly storm the shores of America and China. You also feel with your hearts much of what is not covered in the mass media but objectively exists in the subtle plane of planet Earth.

Yes, you are absolutely right. And indeed, all of this is just a slight and initial manifestation of the events that we warned you about. We have told you that the changes are coming forth, and we have told you that the time has come and the vibrations of the physical plane of the Earth are rising. The Earth is moving up to a new energy level. Now the time has come when these vibrations have direct influence on the physical plane of planet Earth.

We have been so frank with you all this time, and we have warned you about the upcoming events. Why are you surprised?

141

We have given you recommendations for all occasions: how to behave, what to do, and what actions you are to undertake.

Do not say that everything is happening unexpectedly, and that you did not know anything.

Reread our messages that we have been giving through our messenger. Read them carefully through the prism of what is happening in the world now. You will find not only the warnings, but also concrete recommendations on how you should act, how to behave, and how to prepare for what is happening and what is about to happen.

You are in the physical plane, and you are troubled at the start by everything that is happening around you in the physical plane. Yet, we are calling you higher; we are calling you to heavenly peaks, to our world. You will feel yourself in perfect security in our world, under safe control and care.

You are used to the fact that you come into your cozy physical world from embodiment to embodiment. You feel your unbreakable bond with your physical world. You have created this world. I am telling you that the time has come when you should understand and accept in your consciousness that your world will be transformed. For those individuals who have not reached a certain level of consciousness, the current incarnation may be the last manifestation of their individuality in the physical plane.

Think over my words while you still have some time. Accept with your hearts and try to manifest The Great Divine Law in your lives.

All things perishable that have been created by your imperfect consciousness will cease to exist. Only eternal things will remain: the best manifestations of your Spirit, unselfishness, sacrifice, devotion, the highest manifestation of Love, and many other things will exist with you in the New World. When the old world moves to non-existence, the New World will take its place.

There will be no place for any human negative manifestations in this world. Only that which is eternal and represents the manifestation of the best human qualities will remain in this world. And these qualities will multiply and grow. All the obsolete will be swept away and destroyed.

You have nothing to worry and grieve about. Trust the Great Law of the Universe. Nothing will happen to those who believe, to those who love, to those who have hope. Believe me.

I am with you. All the Ascended Hosts are with you. We will give our help all the way to everyone who still has the Divine Monad and in whom the Divine essence is manifested.

None of our people are to fall into non-existence. Everything will be as it is written in the Sacred Books of the past and present.

God is with you! Do not be afraid of the changes!

**I AM Sanat Kumara. Om.**

# The New Day has come

## December 20, 2008

I AM Sanat Kumara. I have come again in order to affirm the consciousness of Victory in your hearts! <...>

<...>

We are telling you that the New Day is coming on planet Earth. And that day will be much happier than everything in the history of humanity for the whole visible historical.

Do not be afraid of the difficulties that are caused by those changes. All old and useless things will have to be taken to the garbage heap of history. All the impeding things will have to be taken away from the Path and burned in the cosmic stove.

However, we widely open the doors of the cosmic opportunity for the individuals who are ready for these changes, who are tired of living in the conditions of the cloaca of the existing civilization.

Welcome to the radiant tomorrow! Do not forget, however, that this radiant tomorrow will be built with your help, with your hands and feet, and with the aspiration of your hearts!

We just show you the Path and the direction according to which humanity should develop further. You must accept our Teaching and the principles of building the New World in your hearts. And then the whole planet will move to the New Day by collective efforts.

The old world will be off and away in the near future. The doors of the cosmic opportunity are wide open. Yet, be so kind as to pass through the doors with your head high, your shoulders straightened, and accompany your procession with joyful smiles.

You must understand that when a new Divine opportunity is given, there comes a time when all the old institutions established by mankind in the last centuries should be reorganized to conform to the new principles; otherwise they will be swept away as useless trash, and the new ways of managing the society will appear in their place. You should never cling to the old and obsolete. We teach you to be ready for constant changes, for continual consonance with the Higher worlds. Only those of you who are not afraid of the changes will be able to adapt smoothly to the new conditions which are coming into the world now. And those of you who cling to the habits of the past and to their past attachments, those who are not ready for the changes, you will have to go through very hard times. Unfortunately, we do not have any more time to wait for the laggards. We are accelerating the speed of our transformations of planet Earth.

If you reread every single dictation carefully, you will find very many keys and useful information there on how you should act in that hard transient time.

Do not be lazy. Do understand that only reading of our messages is not enough; you should thoroughly follow the advice and all the recommendations given by us in your lives. And then it will be much easier to withstand and pass all the tests that are coming forth and have just started.

You have very little time. That is why you should make it a rule to put into practice at least one of our recommendations every day and to utter at least one of the prayer-calls given by us.

If you do not take at least one little step forward, you fall behind more and more, and you risk missing the Divine opportunity that is opening up.

We are running at top speed! We are ready for the changes that are happening. It is your turn now.

Awake those who are still asleep. It is time to wake up, the New Day is outside.

**I AM Sanat Kumara, and I have been with you.**

# Stop evading the tasks of evolution

## June 20, 2009

I AM Sanat Kumara, having come to you again today. I am happy that I have an opportunity to give messages to the Earth's humanity. We are not always afforded such an opportunity, as the situation on the Earth changes and the consciousness of individuals is subject to changes to a great extent.

I have come today in order to give you an idea of what is happening on the planet. Many of you, watching the situation around you in the physical plane, think about what is going on. Everything seems to be as usual but still has somehow subtly altered. Moreover, it seems to many of you that the whole world has gone mad. And this will not be far from the truth.

Really, we laid our account with a bigger transformation of the consciousness of people. We reckoned on an opportunity for a greater cooperation when we started to work through our messenger in Russia. Now we are watching with surprise the repetition of the sad experience of America. The Russian people

147

have taken the same tack. They wonder at the messages, look upon them as at an oddity, and our messages and our Teaching only occupy their consciousness for as long as the time necessary for the reading of a dictation.

Unfortunately, we have not yet gotten what we expected. We do not see readiness for cooperation. We do not see those individuals who are to such extent permeated with our Teaching that they are ready to sacrifice everything they have, to sacrifice their very life in order for their unselfish service for the good of the evolutions of planet Earth to turn the consciousness of many people living on the planet in the direction of knowing the Divine Truth.

We have realized that our hopes have again fallen short of our expectations. We have again encountered the lethargy of human consciousness and its unpredictability. Well, we have drawn our lessons and are ready to continue the movement on the path of evolutionary development. For you, hope remains; but in order for that hope to come true, you should think hard about whether you are doing everything the way you that should do it.

Since the situation on the planet is heating up, we do not have any more time to say too much and speak for a long time. We draw on the Teaching which has been given already. And in order for you to continue moving, you should devote every day of your life to the change of your consciousness. I understand very well and am aware of the fact that you are immersed in the illusion, and the illusion is increasing more and more with each day.

Do understand us as well. We are concerned and care about the salvation of each soul who is still asleep but hears our call, our exhorting, and our Teaching in his or her doze. You still cannot distinguish whether what you hear from us is a continuation of your dream or already the sounds of a New Day.

However, we are satisfied with a little: you hear us and this already gladdens us.

Never stop aspiring. Never allow the illusion to capture your consciousness completely.

I do not lose hope, and I assure all the cosmic councils that the humanity of planet Earth is able to progress on the evolutionary path of development.

However, there is less and less time left. I will not disclose the terms that are being discussed and the dates of the impending events. What good will this do for you?

For those who have been sleeping there will be no significance in what is going to happen. For those who are awakened no harm will come to them.

Only those few are remaining who hear my words as if in a doze and forget about them immediately after reading my message.

But even for you I will not disclose the terms because the time does not matter at all if you don't manage to master the transformation of your consciousness now.

I have come to remind you that now very much, if not everything depends on each of you who are in embodiment.

Stop evading the tasks of evolution, stop hiding in your safe nooks and continuing secretly to play your childish games. You have already grown out of all the possible limits when it was necessary for you to master our Teaching.

Now I have to tell you with full responsibility that the whole world and its destiny depend on those few who have come into embodiment exactly in this time with a definite mission and goal but who have been carried away with games in the illusion to such an extent that they have missed all the given deadlines. We are facing the need to either extend the terms or make you awaken from your lethargy by force.

Every time we talk and warn you, and every time your consciousness refuses to believe that everything is very serious. Let this message of mine make you open your eyes at least for a while and see the danger that is threatening mankind if it is not able, in the face of those few who have come into embodiment exactly for this purpose, to do what the Cosmic Law requires to be done now. And now it is required to prove that mankind is capable of cooperation with the Higher Worlds, that mankind can and wants to develop and follow the ascending path of evolutionary development.

I am telling you all this openly and earnestly because I have taken upon myself a responsibility for mankind of earth. And I will continue waking you up and forcing you to awaken until you do this.

You cannot imagine how difficult it is for me to convince the Great Central Sun that mankind needs a little more time and a little more energy. It is a pity that you cannot appreciate and understand the care and guardianship that your senior brothers and sisters, the Ascended Masters, are rendering to you now.

I will be silent now because everything that I have told requires time for thinking it over. Do promise me that you will reread this message of mine at least three times in different states of your consciousness.

I have come to you today in order to make one more attempt to evoke a response from your hearts.

**I AM Sanat Kumara. Om.**

# A warning that you have chosen the most difficult path to the future

## December 1, 2009

I AM Sanat Kumara, having come again.

I have come because I am overwhelmed with the feeling of Love towards humanity. And I am ready to sacrifice all of my attainments, the whole momentum of my attainments so that mankind can live and evolve.

Yes, the question is still very serious. We do our best, and every time we look back at you Earthlings who are incarnated now, we watch what has changed. If it were not for my multi-million experiences with humanity of the Earth, I would have stopped this experiment a long time ago. But over that time I have loved humanity of the Earth and its best representatives so much that I cannot help sacrificing my momentum of attainments for you, Earthlings, time and again.

Actually, I have come in order to announce certain imbalances which we cannot manage to improve by our own efforts. We expected more support from the light-bearers of planet Earth.

When we started the cycles of the dictations through our Messenger in 2005, the Flame of Victory kindled in the hearts of 144,000 of Christ-beings who are incarnated now! We were happy to behold this Flame, blazing up here and there on the planet.

However, in the course of time, daily concerns of life and the lack of aspiration and devotion put out the Flame within these pure souls. And now there are hardly a few hundred light-bearers around the world who are able to keep their momentum of attainments and to share their Light with others.

Where are the other light-bearers? When we started our mission through this Messenger, many souls remembered their Divine mission. A great many of them were attracted by the Teaching being given by us. Among these ones who were attracted, there were even more of those who wished to take advantage of the Light being released. Yes, beloved, imperfection is prevailing in your world. And the first wave of light-bearers, attracted to the new source of the Teaching, dissolved in the sea of those who only wished to receive without giving anything in return.

It is a pity that among many, many light-bearers nobody was found who would be able to overpower external and internal resistance and to withstand this unequal battle. I am talking about the battle, using military terminology, because nobody cancels Armageddon, nobody cancels that battle that is being waged for people's souls on the Earth. And the reaping is greater from the opposing side than from the side of the forces of Light.

Our efforts, aimed to arrange the location in the physical plane where the light-bearers could combine their efforts and draw their plan of actions have faced an unprecedented resistance. This resistance cannot be compared to the resistance which our Messengers faced in the past. Yes, we are able to act in the territory of Russia, but the darkness, having attacked our outpost in the physical plane from all sides, surpassed all our expectations. We did not expect and we did not take measures because the main attacks that took place there came not from the forces of the dark but from those people who considered themselves the light-bearers — or they were the light-bearers until recently.

What do we see now? We see dissension, rumors, and gossip. We see censure and stench. All our efforts face the resistance, unprecedented resistance in people's hearts and minds.

The time has speeded up. The time has speeded up greatly, and that sad picture that we can observe in our old organizations around the world has been manifested in the territory of Russia within just a year.

We are sorry about the wasted energy. This energy could go for the creation of a brilliant future for Russia. And now all this energy is lying as viscous treacle on the territory of Ashram, here and there throughout Russia, where the former light-bearers sow discord and doubts instead of sowing Light, Love, and Hope.

I have something to say to our Messenger in this respect. However, I don't know anyone who is incarnated now, who in his or her shoes would be able to withstand such attacks from the front and from behind, from the light-bearers, and from government institutions and structures.

Yes, beloved, before you gain the right to guide people, the whole of Russia and all of its authorities and structures must pass tests; the same goes for the judiciary, the legislative authorities, and the inspecting authorities. However, our main failure was exactly in the light-bearers who turned from the eagle chicks of my nest into a flock of crows within just a few years. I grieve and I am very sorry to see this and to be aware of all this.

We saw the other path, the heavenly path. Nevertheless, mankind still tends to go along the most difficult way. Well, we respect your choice.

However, when your sufferings, sorrows, and troubles will exceed all imaginable limits, you should know that there are the Ascended Masters who are always ready to extend their helping hand to you.

We are always ready for cooperation. We are always ready to render help. Your karma does not always allow us to give the help, but this is what you have created yourselves, and the Law of Karma keeps working inviolably in the Universe.

In order for the easy heavenly path to open again, we need the manifestation of your inner attainments. Your inner choices determine the future of mankind which may change any moment if only a certain number of the light-bearers manifest their oneness and aspiration.

Every time you have to start in more and more severe conditions. You have to overpower all those karmic loads that you created yourselves.

In all honesty, can you say that all your efforts, all your energy, all your aspirations for the last few years have been applied by you only for the service to the Great White Brotherhood? How many of you can honestly answer this question affirmatively?

So, what do you expect from the future then? How can we evaluate your degree of willingness and your attainments if today you eagerly follow the direction that we show you, and tomorrow you will go in the opposite direction, or even prefer to spend your time in depression and doing nothing, or descend to the level of playing with the illusory toys of your world?

I have come with this message to give you the explanation of the situation taking place on the Earth now and to warn that you have chosen the most difficult path to the future.

**I AM Sanat Kumara. Om.**

# Call for Awakening

## January 7, 2010

I AM Sanat Kumara. I have come to you again.

Now, when the annual cycle has begun and the session of the Karmic Board has ended, I again have something to talk to you about.

I would like to address those of you who, despite all life hardships and misfortunes, are striving to maintain your consciousness directed to God.

I would like to address those of you who are capable of overcoming difficulties and at the same time preserving your level of consciousness.

It is a very valuable quality. There was a time when you studied at our mystery schools. At that time it was a specially organized practice when you were brought into the state of instability and imbalance to see how you could preserve inner peace and your devotion to fulfilling the Will of God on the Earth.

It was training before your present incarnation. Now it is not necessary to purposefully organize difficulties.

The difficulties that surround you are enough. And now a very important moment of your incarnation has come, when you should not only maintain your consciousness at the highest level available to you, but you also have to do work for the Brotherhood.

You do not need to be told what kind of work you have to do. It is enough to look around and you will see that the entire world needs to be remodeled at the present moment. There is no single area of human activity that would comply with the Divine models.

You probably think that I am calling you to roll up your sleeves and run to change the whole order that exists on Earth.

I think that, most likely, you would be perceived as a crazy person, although, from our point of view, the whole mankind has gone mad and is doing unimaginable things. However, at this stage mankind is not able to comprehend that.

You can talk as much as you want about the Divine principles of the society and about the Divine models that need to be instilled in all spheres of life.

I do not think that there are even several people in your circles who would be able to understand you, and more so, would start to actually do something.

So what should be done and what solution do the Ascended Masters offer?

I have said many times and am now repeating our principles that we have been following for millions of years.

You should begin to change yourselves. Everything around you will be protesting. Since your vibrations will be changing, sooner or later they will begin to contradict the vibrations of the surrounding world. That is when you need to remember the mystery schools once again. Your task is to withstand the unfriendly attitudes of the outside world; by doing so, you will be growing your spiritual muscles and demonstrating your devotion to the work of the Masters regardless of the outer conditions.

How much time will you have to withstand that? You should be prepared to do that until the end of your current incarnation.

There are also those among you who have incarnated with a certain mission. This mission is to create a model in the physical plane of Earth where the Masters could carry out their principles.

Presently, I do not know where on Earth it will be possible to create such a place. We tried to create such a place based on the Ashram of our Messenger. But now I am telling you that we have withdrawn that task from her.

The opposition that we encountered was too strong. That is why at the present time we are looking for another place where we could create our outpost in the physical plane.

The Messenger cannot do the work for those of you who have come into the incarnation and are now quietly lying on the couch.

We have been observing the heroic efforts of our Messenger for two years. And now we clearly see that we can no longer exploit her devotion and self-sacrifice.

That would be wrong. And, if there is nobody in the physical plane that could take care of our Messenger and protect her, then I will do that.

For I have a special relationship with this Messenger. And it was I who vouched for her before her incarnation.

I can no longer risk my favorite disciple.

You will now have to do everything yourselves, provided that you can handle the load that will inevitably come upon you as soon as you begin to do work for the Brotherhood — the real work for the Brotherhood and not the work that you imagine for yourselves.

Today again I have been quite harsh.

I was able to be present in the body of the Messenger many times during her meetings with numerous people. I understand very well that she tried to maintain a blameless perception of everyone as we had taught her, but I clearly saw everyone who approached the messenger throughout these years. And, because you have come into my visual field, I will be able to do everything I can in order to either impart wisdom to you or to leave you up to the will of karma.

I am not speaking about those who approached to taste the Light. There were also those, whom I knew personally, and who had to take on certain functions. You had gone through a special training; we nurtured and cherished your souls before their incarnation, and we did everything we could in order to put together the outer circumstances and bring you close to our Messenger. And what is the result?

You cannot feel the depth of my frustration that I am experiencing. I can only observe everything that is happening. Yet, I cannot interfere, as you have your free will and are free to do everything that you want.

God forbid that you experience my state in which I see how one person after another makes a choice in favor of illusion. We are losing the best ones, the most devoted ones. Not a single mission of Light has ever been based on one person. There have always been many souls who came into incarnation. Some of them got lost in the beginning of the incarnation, but the rest could closely approach the fulfillment of their mission by means of strenuous efforts. And now I see how each of them has chosen his or her toy and has run to chase his or her goal in the illusionary world.

We have attained a new dispensation, new Divine mercy for transmitting this new cycle of messages into your world. And I truly hope that those who are still wandering in the illusion will be able to hear the call that is contained in these messages and awaken their consciousness to action.

Otherwise, you will continue to wander alone in the illusion until the end of your current incarnation.

There is a Divine opportunity that is still not over. But where are those light bearers with whose hands and feet we could fulfill our plans?

**I AM Sanat Kumara. Om.**

# A Teaching on responsibility

**June 1, 2010**

I AM Sanat Kumara, coming to you through our messenger again.

I have come today to remind you of the current situation on the planet again and of your responsibility for the situation on the Earth. When humankind is able to realize the whole fullness of responsibility for everything that happens on the Earth, we will be able to breathe with relief. So long as humankind has the consciousness level of a child, we are forced to take care of it and watch that the children of the Earth, because of their thoughtlessness, don't make such a mess that life on the planet becomes impossible.

And now that I have alerted you a little to my understanding of the situation on the planet, I am ready to give a small Teaching that will be useful for you to listen to.

Because your consciousness cannot concentrate on something specific for a long time, we have to come many times to remind you of very simple truths which you probably know but for some reason have forgotten to put into practice and hold in your consciousness.

I have come after a long break in our work with humankind of the Earth through this messenger. And all that time I had an opportunity to watch the development of events on the planet from the fine plane. You also had an opportunity to watch the development of events but only from your physical plane. And those people who are thoughtful and analytical could notice that the situation on the planet becomes more strained every day. And practically ceaseless earthquakes, volcanic eruptions, military conflicts, acts of terrorism, social explosions, and coups that happen here and there on the globe give clues about the situation on the planet.

It seems to you that it is natural and there is nothing unusual in it. Indeed, all those features of undeveloped human consciousness have existed before. They existed one hundred and several hundred years ago. But the frequency and the scale of those negative phenomena and those negative forces that stand behind those phenomena have never been so large.

Let me tell you that my memory is much better than the memory of currently incarnated humans of the Earth. And I have an opportunity to look into the chronicles of akasha and compare your situation with any of the situations that have ever existed on the Earth. The result of that comparison won't be in favor of the current situation. We, the Ascended Realm, need more and more energy to hold the situation on the planet, to not permit the most horrible occurrence for humankind, in which the physical platform itself would become destroyed.

It seems to you that I speak about something that has no immediate reference to you, as if somebody's actions somewhere else led to the imbalance on the Earth and that manifested in volcanic eruptions and tornadoes.

Beloved, do not think so categorically. All currently incarnated individuals on the Earth are so closely interwoven with their karma that it is impossible to distinguish who and what action led to a catastrophe that is going on now on the Earth.

The informational field of humankind relates more and more to the general informational field in which it is impossible to pick out the contribution of a separate individual. The development of modern mass media led to the fact that the news reaches the most distant places on the globe in a fraction of a second. And every man that resonates on the news makes his contribution in the energy situation on the Earth.

Not all of the news draws a wide response. And most information is hidden from humankind because if humankind knew all the information about the destroying impacts of all that is happening on the planet now, the resonance in the minds of people will have an uncontrolled character.

Your weak memory and inability to realize the whole burden of the current situation on the planet is actually quite fortunate for you.

A very lofty consciousness is needed that can hold the existing entire imbalance on the planet and balance it with their own inner achievements. I will let you in on a secret that there are a definite number of incarnated individuals who undertake the task of balancing the energies on the planet. And it is thanks to those selfless souls that the earth has an opportunity to exist.

However, those of you who are reading these lines now need to spend more time in the inner work over yourselves, for only because of your inner achievements is it possible to balance the situation at every point of the planet where you live.

There are certain people who are continuing to rock the boat under their own ignorance. But those very people waste the last crumbs of their good karma, littering the informational field of the planet even more.

Every low-grade thought of yours is multiplied by millions of times. You can watch the analog of that process in the Internet. There are a lot of places in that virtual space where a man, often under a fictitious name, says ridiculous things, flagrantly lies, or talks nonsense. And you can see how quickly thousands of simpletons flock together on that "news" and spread it all over the Internet.

That is how you create karma not noticing it without being aware of your actions. One of the basic and cornerstone Teachings that was given by us through our messenger is the Teaching on the careful attitude towards spending the Divine Energy. You are responsible for every erg of the Divine Energy that you receive from the Divine World. And the way that you consume the Divine Energy weaves either an immortal body of Light for you or a web that ties you to the physical plane of the Earth forever and closes your opportunity for further growth in the finer and loftier worlds.

Today I have given the Teaching that reminds you of your responsibility. And I think that in the current situation on the planet it won't do any harm to listen to that Teaching once again.

**I AM Sanat Kumara. Om**

# An urgent message

## November 16, 2010

I AM Sanat Kumara. I have come again today to give a talk that is necessary; and I think that many of you who are reading these lines will probably be puzzled. However, the time is pressing. Therefore, I am going to start.

We have not been giving any dictations through our messenger lately. And that is quite righteous, as there is no point in giving the Knowledge to those who cannot perceive and adopt this Knowledge.

The purpose and the reason for my coming today is to apply to those few who are incarnated and can hear me. I am appealing to you.

There are few of you; and the circumstances of life become more and more aggravating. The karma of humanity becomes dense and draws in all those who are forced to follow the overall mass of people.

You have to stop. Let the crowd of people be noisy, but may the fuss within your being calm down.

It is your turn. You have incarnated for the mission, the time for which is coming.

You are to step out of the crowd; you are to separate yourselves and to become those who you really are – the transmitters of Light, the electrodes of Light. Through you, through your conductors, the balancing of planet Earth must be carried out.

Severe times are approaching. And there are only several people in incarnation that can perform this work for us.

The fuss of life is to subside. Everything is to be silent within you. Your time has come. And now, when I have prepared you for the perception, I must tell you one more thing, the main thing: all of you are becoming active collaborators of the Brotherhood on the Earth. And I am speaking for you now. You should focus on the inner work of balancing the situation on the planet.

There is no other way. Never has the situation been so heavy on the planet.

The balance must be restored, at the cost of prayers, at the cost of setting inner peace and silence.

There are few of you, and it is only possible to maintain the balance by an incredible concentration on the inner work, by concentration on the Supreme during all day.

Do not pay attention to that what is happening around you. Concentrate only on the heart, on God residing within you.

Let the wind blow, let there be a snowstorm, let the conflagrations rage, let the world collapse; if within at least several people the flame is burning smoothly, and peace and harmony are reigning, everything can still be changed.

I am calling upon you to keep silent. I am calling upon you to pray. I am calling upon you to meditate. I am calling upon you to become those who you really are: the sons and the daughters of God. Everything will fall silent within you and the balance will gradually revive.

And now I am ready to tell you one more thing: do not be afraid of anything. All the worst things that could happen have already happened. The rest will be just a consequence of what has happened. Today I have come in order for those who are ready to hear me to carry out their duty.

**I AM Sanat Kumara. Om.**

# The moment of your final choice has come

## December 22, 2010

I AM Sanat Kumara, having come to you again.

The grace of Heaven is truly infinite.

Every time I come to start the message, I am pleased with the opportunity that opens and tremble with joy.

Now, after that small introduction, I am ready to give the next message. Many souls are looking forward to the news from Heaven as to a gift and a sign of the fact that the Heavens have not left humanity of the Earth.

Beloved, of course, we cannot leave our child in the lurch.

O, thousands of Light Beings take so much care of you! Those who are incarnated can hardly believe it because you do not see us. But believe me, the veil between our worlds becomes thinner, though it may seem strange to many of you. And sometimes you only have to change your view of what is happening just a bit, and what is usually hidden from people's eyes will be revealed to you. The perspective of further development will be opened to you. And of course, that perspective is not connected to the achievements of your science and technology. However, it is exactly the development of your science and technology that facilitates your consciousness to direct to the finer planes of being.

The seeming contradiction is quite explainable and is not a contradiction at all from our point of view. When you strain your mind with the things that are impossible for you to touch but that you can see only in your imagination, you are getting used to dealing with the finer reality from the plane of thoughts. And gradually, new technologies make humanity shift the focus of their perception of reality to the finer fields.

It seems to you that you are constantly in your physical body. Yes, you see the things around and you can touch them, but most of the time of day, including the time of your nightly dream, you stay on the other planes of being. My example will give you understanding of what is meant. When you think about a person who is thousands of kilometers away from you, you contact him on the finer plane of being. There are no distances for thoughts and feelings.

Only as a consequence of your conductors being coarsened, you cannot feel the interactions of the finer planes of being. There are several people who purposefully use the work of the thought even at this time. However, such work doesn't always lead to a positive result and it creates karma more often, as the motive of those people is not always pure. The only true motives which you should follow in any of your actions in any planes of being are Mercy, Compassion, unmercenariness, and your wish to help Life. All other motives will not be pure enough and will lead to an incorrect result or fruit.

It will be easier for you to understand what I am speaking about if I give one more example. Imagine that using the method you have been given at some regular seminar or training you will build a happy future for you and your family by your thought. "What is so bad about that?" you will ask.

There is nothing so bad in your wish to live happily from the human point of view. However, the wish is the basis of your action. In this case, it is your wish to live happily. The wish is the manifestation of your inferior nature. So you get under the influence of your inferior nature. And consequently, all the actions that you will perform will create karma.

True Teachings given by the initiates teach the abandonment of wishes as one of the manifestations of the inferior nature of a human.

You attach yourself to the physical world more and more while your wishes rule your actions. And you know that the physical world is the lowest of the worlds. So, attaching to it you doom yourself to further incarnations. True Teachings teach how you can free yourself from the wheel of sansara.

The illusion becomes more and more refined and, as you have reason, you should constantly analyze the situations you face and make sensible choices.

Each of your decisions either moves you along the way to the Higher Worlds or makes you slide down the descending spiral. And the motive that drives you while making a decision, in fact, determines the direction of your moving.

On the one hand, you abandon wishes, personal motives, and in terms of an average common human consciousness you are said to be a loser or a strange person. Believe me, that from the other point of view, you make huge steps along the way of the evolution. Other people who seem successful in all respects, who get all possible pleasures from life, keep rolling down away from evolutionary development.

That is the fundamental test of your time. On the one hand, there is a bright wild illusion that unfolds anew, charming your imagination and alluring sides in front of you. On the other hand, there is the ancient Teaching that teaches us to abandon illusion in order to acquire eternal values.

Ninety percent of people will prefer what seems real to them, what gives them pleasure, the pleasure of possession and the pleasure for their senses. And only 10 percent will think that if the ancient Teachings taught the abandonment of illusion, then perhaps there is something in it and it is worth listening to. And only several percent of those people who rush along the true spiritual path are able to acquire the necessary distinction and pass tests to have the right to move up to the other evolutionary turn.

Today I have not taught you anything new that haven't been mentioned before, either in the dictations that we gave through our messenger or in those true Teachings that were given in ancient times.

The difference is that you won't be able to pretend anymore that nothing is happening and that you have much time for your spiritual growth ahead.

There is no time left. The moment of your final choice has now come. I am always ready to lend my helping hand to help those who have chosen the Path which the Ascended Masters teach.

**I AM Sanat Kumara. Om.**

# Keep your consciousness at the level where it is invulnerable to the temptations of the illusion

**June 14, 2011**

I AM Sanat Kumara.

On this day, I have come to you again in order to talk about the essential, about what interests you and what we wish to deliver to your consciousness at this current moment in time.

I would like to add to this introduction that at the current moment there is no task that is more important for us, the Ascended Hosts, than awakening the best representatives of mankind incarnated now from their centuries-old sleep. I hold personal responsibility for many of you. That is because our close bonds rooting back into the remote past oblige me to render all the help to your souls that can be rendered. First and foremost, it is the help with the awakening of your souls.

When your soul awakens to the higher reality, you resemble a person who wakes up and is ready for the hustles of the New Day. Your consciousness begins to take in those Truths which were inaccessible for it even the day before. It is because the veil becomes thinner as if somebody waved the magic wand.

In the same way it is happening now. We are seizing the cosmic moment that allows us to very carefully, with light and with almost imperceptible touches, awaken your souls from the sleep.

We are directing our energies of awakening into the surrounding space continuously and tirelessly. And now I am focusing my energies for those who are ready for awakening.

The whole diversity of the surrounding reality requires your constant attention and concentration on the physical world around you. It is not the same with my energies — they make you direct your attention at the world which is invisible to your physical senses but yet you suspect its existence. And you know that sooner or later this world will become as familiar, close, and dear to you as your physical world is now.

However, do not be in a rush to get into our world as soon as possible. That is because in order to exist at another level of consciousness, you will need to learn a lot. Therefore, do not waste your time during your incarnation. Develop those qualities and gain those skills that you will need in our world, the New World, into which you should inevitably transition.

Prepare your conduits for the perception of a more subtle reality. Always remember that your physical reality will try to hold you, as soon as you start aspiring to the higher worlds. Such is the law of the matter. Such is the law of this Universe. The old and the obsolete that must give way to the new will resist. The resistance of the matter increases with the coming of the New Time. You feel it in yourself and in your environment. At times, the situation seems to have become absurd, and it becomes obvious for everybody that it cannot continue in that way anymore. There cannot be a deadlock on the path of evolution. The way out must be found!

Beloved, you should slightly change your angle of vision in order to see the germs of the New World, new consciousness and new relationships behind all the negative manifestations which overfill your world.

All that you need for further development already exists in your world. However, the illusion, due to the inevitable law, keeps throwing new obstacles on your Path. At present, a main obstacle is the diversity of information that literally fills the Internet space and mass media. One must find the grains of Truth in this ocean of information. It is those grains that should form a harmonious belief system in your consciousness.

I understand you and your difficulties very well. However, there is a criterion, which by using you can and must find those grains of information that you need at this stage. In order to find these grains of Truth, you absolutely do not need to search through all the garbage that lies on the shelves of bookstores and floods the television and radio space of the Earth and the Internet.

You should pay more attention to your inner world and your inner sensations. If you are attuned with the Divine Truth inside yourselves, then this tuning-fork sound of your soul will attract the necessary information to you from the surrounding space while those information surrogates that have filled your world will not draw your attention or divert you from your Path.

Beloved, there is no task that is more important now than getting rid of informational garbage.

Maya[8] in its powerlessness throws more and more new temptations to you. You must carefully distinguish these temptations of the illusion from the real manifestations of the Divine world.

The key to the distinction is your attunement with us, the Ascended Hosts, with the Divine world.

Therefore, always keep your consciousness at the level where it becomes invulnerable to any temptations of the illusion and the arrows of Mara's[9] army.

---

[8] "Mâyâ (Sk.). Illusion; the cosmic power which renders phenomenal existence and the perceptions thereof possible. In Hindu philosophy that alone which is changeless and eternal is called reality; all that which is subject to change through decay and differentiation and which has therefore, a beginning and an end is regarded as mâyâ — illusion." (From *The Theosophical Glossary (1918) [1892]. Mead, George R. S., ed. Los Angeles: Theosophical Publishing Society.* http://www.blavatskycardiff. care4free.net/Blavgloss1892.htm)

[9] "Mara (Sk.). The god of Temptation, the Seducer who tried to turn Buddha away from his Path." (Ibid.)

Your consciousness is very important, and that is why we pay so much attention to your training.

The towrope of the Divine opportunity that we are throwing to you in the form of these messages can pull you out of the sea of illusion. However, you have to apply your own efforts as well, at least to grab this towrope and hold it tightly in your hands.

If you lose your concentration and get carried away by another illusion, you are running the risk of either putting off your advancement on the Path for a long period of time or getting completely lost in the illusionary world. Therefore, maintain your aspiration; always keep the focus in your consciousness on the best, Divine models.

I want to warn you that the presentation of information in your mass media is directed exactly so as to deprive you of the opportunity to concentrate your attention on one object for a considerably long period of time. Yet, without the skill of concentration it is impossible for you to overcome the resistance of the illusion at the present moment in history.

I came today in order to give instructions to those souls who are karmically connected with me. I hold personal responsibility for taking you out of the captivity of the illusion to the expanses of the Universe.

**I AM Sanat Kumara. Om.**

# All opportunities are open in your time

## December 27, 2011

I AM Sanat Kumara.

I have come today, as always, at the end of the annual cycle in order to give the necessary comprehension of the further Path, to strengthen you on your Path, and to bring home to your consciousness those points that you need to your further advancement.

Thus, today we will continue the talk about the Path of Initiations, about how this Path of Initiations of your time differs from the Path of Initiations that was known to humanity in ages past.

You know that in the past times only a very small percent of the incarnated humanity had a notion about the Path of Initiations and had access to the knowledge that is necessary on this Path.

Now the time has changed. Now humanity is on the cusp of the new stage of its development. Greater openness and greater freedom are characteristic of this stage. And we come and give you the knowledge, which was hidden from humanity under the veil of secrecy just a while ago, openly and freely.

The time has come when almost all the knowledge is available and accessible on the bookshelves and on the Internet.

However, the peculiarity of the coming age is connected with the fact that the true knowledge opens to people similarly as the knowledge and the information which are not true but which are the fruit of the mental speculation and consideration of the carnal mind.

Divine wisdom and speculations of the carnal mind are lying side by side on the shelves of bookshops, and then they move to the bookshelves that you have at home.

How safe is it for the development of your souls, and is it reasonable in terms of evolution?

Let us turn to an example.

Small children are protected by their parents against any false steps and any threatening danger. Matches and prickly sharp things are taken away from them so that they cannot hurt themselves. Then the moment comes when the children grow up and start their exploration of the surrounding world. In this case, it is more difficult for the parents to control their children because they come out in the street, go to school, and get on the Internet. What they see and face there slips their parents' attention.

Now the moment has come when humanity grows out of its childish state of consciousness and moves to the world of adults.

However, not everything in this world conforms to the Divine patterns. And many things are the opposite of the Divine world.

How can one make a distinction and discern? Wise parents do not hasten to familiarize their children with the wonders of modern technologies or with the achievements of modern civilization. From the beginning, wise parents try to give their children the idea of the moral law and of the inner guidelines. Wise parents hasten to provide their children with the wisdom of the heart. Then, when a person has the right guidelines within himself, they will lead him through life as a sound of a tuning fork. And what is not consistent with the sound of the tuning fork of his heart will go past his external consciousness without leaving a trace in his soul.

Buddha goes through life quietly, not noticed by anybody, and no mud of life is attached to the golden robe of his aura.

Likewise, we try to give you the right guidelines that will lead you through your life, showing the direction and protecting you. Then, when there is a sensation of reality, Divinity within you, everything that is less than the Divine perfection will go past your consciousness, leaving no traces in it. And you will aspire to your Victory, to your Freedom from the chains of matter.

Those human individuals, who do not have that feeling of the Divine that sounds like a tuning fork within them, are forced to learn their lessons of life in order to gain that distinction and comprehension that are needed for further evolution. And life offers rich and diverse material for your development.

The refinement of the illusion and of its facets makes you develop your distinction and gain merits on this path of distinction.

There are also other people who do not wish to burden themselves with any effort, who see the surrounding world only as a source of satisfaction of their desires and needs.

Well, this group of people is also given an opportunity to satisfy all their desires and all their aspirations in order that, once having been tired of the race for knick-knacks and pleasures, they could stop and raise their look towards timeless reality.

There is a definite amount of time in order for each human individual to reach the border beyond which the real world of God begins. Everyone is given a chance.

And all opportunities are open in your time.

All the processes are accelerating, including the processes of your choices.

And when you persist and continue wandering about the illusion, choosing one toy after another while it is time for you to start doing the deeds of the adults, your mistakes and errors will be pointed out, first in a mild way and then in a clearer and a more insistent way. Everyone is given a chance. Everyone is shown the Path.

And if you were not so involved in your illusory processes and could observe your life from a higher visual angle, you would be able to understand and to perceive how carefully your souls are protected.

However, there is the law of free will that inviolably governs in this universe and on your planet. And none of the Ascended Masters can help you if, of your own free will, you have been choosing the world liable to decay from embodiment to embodiment, for tens and hundreds of thousands of years.

Sooner or later the term of the experiments in the earthly reality will be over for those individuals. And like pupils left back in school they will be forced to continue their education but in another reality. Millions and billions of years of evolution will be provided for them again.

For those, who heed our guidance, the days of staying in the illusory world will be reduced. Unprecedented opportunities are opening up for you, for your spiritual growth and advancement along the path of evolution that the Ascended Masters, the Masters of Wisdom, teach.

We are always beside you at the most slippery parts of the Path. Just wish and you will be able to start communicating with us directly.

You just need a skill to leave the surrounding illusion for the Divine reality. And nothing is needed for that except for your inner efforts. Like sportsmen train their physical muscles in order to win the competition, you need to train the muscles of your soul in order to achieve your Victory on the Path of Initiations.

With our help, your aspiration and your daily spiritual practices will inevitably raise you to the next evolutionary stage.

I was happy to give you my helping hand today and to give the right direction to your aspirations.

**I AM Sanat Kumara. Om.**

# I wish you to acquire that degree of awareness which will enable you to aspire along the highest Path

**June 21, 2012**

I AM Sanat Kumara, having come to you again.

The worlds, the stars, and the Heavens are rejoicing at the unprecedented opportunity that has opened again thanks to the Mercy of God.

I have come to you today, on the day of the summer solstice, in order to intensify my energies and in order for you to feel our Unity, the Unity of every particle of life with our Heavenly Father, One and inseparable.

This unprecedented cosmic opportunity has become manifested after the decision was reached today at the session of the Karmic Board and after the following affirmation of it on the Great Central Sun, the Sirius star.

I have not come in order for you to get a chance to read another Message. I have come for you to become aware of your Divine mission. Mere reading of our Messages is too little for your stage of evolutionary development. You must apply all your efforts so that your consciousness can take in the Divine Truths. And one of these Truths is that your planet is changing its vibrations. This change opens an opportunity for you to follow the Divine Path of development.

You have become more mature. You have prepared to make the next step in your evolutionary development. Literally yesterday, the Karmic Board and the Supreme Council of this Universe hesitated whether to give or not to give a new opportunity to continue the given dispensation. And so, today the decision has been made! It is necessary to say that literally each movement of your soul, not just your deeds and actions, during the preceding difficult months were verified on the cosmic scales.

We had to state the fact about the great resistance from the opposing forces. And we must take into account the efforts being made by a few souls. The scales have been equalized, and it has required very little for the Divine opportunity to continue. I have volunteered to help. And thanks to my momentum of attainments that I have pledged in the cosmic bank, other Masters and I have acquired an opportunity to come again and give Messages to mankind of the Earth.

This opportunity is not deserved by mankind. And it is now given to you in advance. Therefore, you must constantly keep in mind the fact that in the nearest future each action, each thought or feeling of yours can determine the further fate of the world.

When you take a loan in a bank, you take a risk that you may not repay it. I have vouched for you that you will be able to fulfill the obligations that you have taken upon yourselves before the incarnation. I wish you to acquire the degree of awareness that will enable you to aspire along the highest Path.

Beloved, just a few individuals manifesting the new consciousness and new thinking are enough. It is very difficult, but it is indispensable to be done, for as soon as a few people become able to manifest the new type of relationships based on the new consciousness and new thinking, millions of other people will be able to use this momentum of attainments. The collective unconsciousness of mankind is able to accumulate not only negative manifestations of human consciousness, but also positive aspirations of particular individuals. Therefore, one person capable of manifesting the necessary level of consciousness in these difficult conditions sacrifices his attainments on the altar of Service for mankind. And the whole mankind acquires an opportunity for the further evolution.

This is the principle, and this is the Path. Each of those who achieved a certain level of consciousness in the past was making the path for mankind for hundreds and thousands of years ahead. Two thousand years have passed since the time of the incarnation of Jesus; even more time has passed since the moment of incarnation of Gautama Buddha, but mankind is still using their momentum of attainments.

Each of you is able to demonstrate the new consciousness. Each of you is able to rise to the next

188

evolutionary stage to show the example. It is characteristic of the new age that all your attainments will very quickly be spread all over the globe. Each step of yours in the right direction will be unprecedentedly encouraged by the Heavens.

But it is also true that those individuals who have chosen to separate themselves from God will very soon reap the fruits of their negative karma. The things that do not correspond to the new stage of evolutionary Path will be degrading and will vanish from the face of the Earth. The things that correspond to the new stage will prosper thanks to the Divine Mercy.

You see both kinds of manifestations around you. And each of you has an opportunity to choose death or Immortality; life for yourself or life for the Common Good; decay or eternal Life.

It has never been said more clearly and precisely. And this is the call of the time.

I would like to imprint the uttered words with one example. And this example is given by life itself. Now, when the time of my presence is elapsing, I must say that this represents an opportunity for you for eternal life and immortality which is achievable right now. There has never been such an opportunity before in the past times. The worse the abomination of desolation is around you, the greater value your attainments have in the eyes of God.

Take a look at the lotuses blooming on a swamp. Despite fermentation processes and decay reigning around, God manifests the miracle of the flower of Life.

Every one of you is a miracle in the hands of God. Everything is determined only by your consciousness and your aspiration towards the Divinity.

**I AM Sanat Kumara. Om.**

# Now the time has come for you to act

## December 21, 2012

I AM Sanat Kumara. I have come again.

To you who are in embodiment now, we come in order to render you the help which is possible and necessary to render.

Every time before I arrive and open a new Divine dispensation for the transmission of our Messages from the etheric octaves into your dense world, I meditate for a long time and I carefully pick words which can provide the greatest help and support at the given moment. I know that very many of you are waiting for this great grace and visit our site on the Internet many times in order to make sure that God and the Masters have not abandoned you.

Yes, beloved, the harder it becomes for the light-bearers, our disciples, to stay in the physical world, the more desire and aspiration I come with in order to offer my help to those who yearn for liberation, to those who are ready with all their being for the perception of our energies of regeneration that we tirelessly pour into your world and with our Messages as well.

I know that many of you were looking forward to my Message today, and it is due to many reasons. The main reason is that it is harder and harder for the light-bearers to maintain the balance of the physical plane of the planet. This is true, indeed.

Let me remind you of those moments before your incarnation when you were being given recommendations and exhortations.

You must remember your mission.

You must remember it now.

Every time when any burdensome energies of the world try to take control of your being, you must remember that it is your duty not to surrender to those energies. Any negative energies of the past, which are in your world and densely encircle you, are to be surmounted by you with the help of your inner efforts.

It is exactly now when the time has come for you to act. Your inner attainments, which are manifested as the flames of your heart, as the radiance of your aura, and as a halo around your head, must be used by you now. Any negative quality that comes to the surface from within you or comes to you from the surrounding space requires your immediate work on the neutralization of the negativity.

This is the inner work in the plane of thoughts and in the emotional and astral planes. This is the work of your concealed spiritual muscles that you had to develop during all these years when you were reading our Messages.

It is exactly now that you must work. For the future of planet Earth depends on the effectiveness of your work that you are doing now on the surmounting of any negative states.

If you manage to cope with any negativity that is hovering around you and if you surmount any negative states of your consciousness, it will serve as a guarantee that no natural calamity, ecological catastrophe, or social coup will precipitate onto the physical plane.

The subtle work on the transformation of your own consciousness and sub-consciousness is able to prevent any natural calamity.

New Divine mercies will be granted to planet Earth when the Ascended Hosts make sure that there are a sufficient number of incarnated individuals who can control the space around them and manage the energies in the matter.

Now the time has come for your primary work for which you have come into this embodiment. It is necessary that the balance of energies is constantly maintained with the help of your inner attainments.

Your ego will try to lead you along the wrong path, blaming other people, blaming your governments and authorities. There are always the forces that try to use any negative energy in order to rock the boat more.

A fundamental landmark of our Teaching, which we have been tirelessly giving during the whole history of the development of mankind, is that everything that happens to you happens exactly because you yourselves created the causes of that some time ago.

And as the world is getting more subtle now, there is an opportunity that is opening for you — to cope with any negative energies in the plane of thoughts and feelings before these energies precipitate in the physical plane in the form of hurricanes and cataclysms.

You are given great opportunities for the transformation of the physical plane by means of changing your consciousness.

One person who has attained the level of consciousness of Christ is able to balance the karma of many people with whom he has karmic bonds and with whom he is living in the immediate vicinity. That is why people always treated it with awe if some saint settled in the area where they were living.

They took that knowledge with their mother's milk that the saint who had settled in their area was the guarantor that nothing would happen to their land and their harvest. And their descendants would be healthy and happy.

It is not like that in your time. The world has forgotten the ancient knowledge. And many who pretend to be the saints are not saints, and those who are holy, invoke annoyance and aversion.

As light-bearers you have a primary task to transmit correct guidelines into the world. For this you need to rely on the inner knowledge that comes from within your hearts. For this inner connection with the sacred man of your heart, you need permanent daily work upon yourself and upon your consciousness.

There is a law of tithe that says that one tenth of everything must be given to God. Similarly, a tenth of your time must be given to spiritual practices and God-pleasing deeds.

Do not forget God in the bustle of the day. If in the very prime of the day, when dull energies close up over your head, you are able to keep the memory of God at least in the corner of your consciousness, no storms and stresses of life can threaten you.

Always preserve the purity of your heart, no matter what life situations you are facing. This will help you to keep the right direction in your life and always to follow the higher Path destined for you by God!

**I AM Sanat Kumara. Om.**

# I extend a helping hand to you

**June 20, 2013**

I AM Sanat Kumara.

My fatherly feelings towards humanity of the Earth make me come to you again.

I am experiencing an incomparable trembling at this moment of transmission of My Message. As always, I would like to give you a particle of my consciousness, my comprehension, my faith and my devotion to God and to the Divine Law.

You could receive the whole momentum of my attainments into your aura at that very instant when you read or listen to this Message of Mine. The only obstacle is the resistance of your carnal mind, your ego. You cannot receive when you are not able to accept. And you are not able to accept, for there is an obstacle between you and me in the form of your ego.

Therefore, every time we come, the chief task we set is the surmounting of your ego. We will become able to achieve our Unity and to unite in Spirit only if we make steps towards each other.

I come and I extend a helping hand to you. But you must also make efforts and extend your hand to me.

I tirelessly repeat that it behooves you to steadily work towards our collaboration and our Unity in God to take place. It is impossible for you to follow the Path and our recommendations one day and yield to the passions of your ego the next day. It is impossible for you to be our disciple today and to forget about it tomorrow.

Successiveness and consistency of your actions, your choices, and your efforts — this is what we tirelessly strive for and call you to follow.

Every time when you, inspired by our Messages, make a decision to follow the Path we show, do not forget about this decision of yours the next day.

The resistance of the matter at present has reached its utmost. Therefore, it will require the efforts of your whole being to overpower the illusory forces. And you will be able to do it. You will be able to overpower the resistance of any external and internal negative forces and energies. The only thing you really need is your wish and aspiration, devotion and consistency.

In order to derive these qualities from the innermost of your being, you need a diamond-strong faith based on heartfelt unconditional love to all Creation.

You cannot instantly re-tune your being and attune yourself with the Hierarchy, but you are able to achieve it by making gradual daily steps in the necessary direction. The advice and recommendations we give are sufficient for a determined advancement along your Path back Heavenward.

You only have to constantly remember us, to keep consonance in your hearts. The Brotherhood makes tremendous efforts thereto. Every time we come to give our Messages, millions of the Ascended Hosts render their assistance and contribution during each transmission of the Message. That is why our Messages are the most precious treasure in your world. Our Messages are a materialization of the Divine Energy. Grain by grain within eight and a half years our energy and our vibrations are penetrating into your world.

And we sincerely hope that you will manage to utilize the energy, the knowledge received from us, and the comprehension of the Divine Law adequately and with care.

Every time when you read our Messages, take a minute to think of how great are the efforts made for the transmission of the Messages to your world. And if you could respond to our call with the efforts equal to those we make, the Divine Law would be fulfilled and the energy exchange between our octaves completed. This would prove the ability of the terrestrial evolutions for the further development in God.

However, it does not take place. And you can make sure of that with your own experience.

How long does your readiness and determination that you acquire while reading another Message of ours last? Until the first phone call or the conversation in a chat room with your friends? Until another piece of amusement and pleasure which attract you in your world? Until another movie you watch on television?

You cannot instantly cast away the surrounding illusion, but you are able to make successive steps to overpower it. The Path, which is outstretched before you, opens not beyond yourselves. This Path reveals itself within you. And this Path is the changing of your consciousness.

You run the process of changing your consciousness yourselves. All the external illusion is unfolded before you only to enable you to make your choices and advance along the Path. However, you prefer to descend into the illusion deeper and deeper instead of parting with it.

This is your choice and your decision. There is no being in the whole Universe who would make your choices for you.

And now put yourselves into my place. For millions of years I continue to teach you the fundamentals of the Teaching. I come through many messengers and prophets. I give one and the same Teaching within millions of years. Many of you have heard this Teaching personally from me in the retreats of the Brotherhood and from My messengers for tens and hundreds of times. But then you came in touch with the illusory world, and the Light of your eyes faded, and your determination left you, and you plunged deeper and deeper into the illusion of your world. Then there came a moment when in the last hope you turned your eyes Heavenward and asked for help and salvation. It recurred from life to life, scores of times.

If any of you were in my place, you would have given up on this long ago. However, I bear responsibility for each of you. And I will be coming and giving you my Teaching and my exhortations despite your stubbornness.

I do not know how much more time your soul requires to become fed up with playing in the illusion and to aspire to the Heavenly peaks of the Divine consciousness, but I know that there will come a moment when you will be able to raise your consciousness to such a peak and to see the prospect of the Divine Path of development, and you will turn your eyes away from the glittering trinkets of your world for good.

I wish you to face this moment of clarity already in this incarnation. I wish you to make your step to infinity and come out beyond the boundaries of the illusion fettering you as soon as possible.

I extend my hand to you and patiently wait for you to become able to come and shake it.

**I AM Sanat Kumara. Om.**

# Your world must inevitably change in order to develop further according to the Divine pattern

## December 20, 2013

I AM Sanat Kumara.

I have come to you again, children of Earth.

Every time we come you are offered an opportunity to get in touch with Ancient knowledge concerning the structure of the Universe and your mission here as of a part of the whole Universe.

Yes, beloved, each of you has his special mission within the limits of the whole evolutionary development of this Universe.

At times it is very difficult for you to tolerate and bear delusions that try to conquer you.

The Law of the free will is inviolable in your world. However, there are cosmic terms and there is a corridor of the Divine opportunity. I have come to remind you that the Divine opportunity is getting narrow. And your world is to change inevitably in order to develop further according to the Divine pattern. This is axiomatic. But I have to remind you of this.

I often visit your world to get an impression of the processes that are taking place and to adjust them on time. Still, you have to realize that there is the evolutionary path for your souls made by the Creator of this Universe, and there is that path which most of mankind follow at this time. That road leads nowhere. It is the path of following the inferior, animal-like instincts and your carnal mind.

We cannot force you to give up your choice. You must understand that neither I, nor any other of the Masters will come to you, grab you by the hand like a disobedient child, and by force take you to the Divine Path of development.

This is the mission of your time: to separate those souls that are capable of further evolution from the souls that are to be burnt in the cosmic stove like weeds.

The other Masters and I come to you through our messenger exactly in order to give you this understanding of the processes that are taking place and to show the Path.

You must have more self-sacrifice and to Serve Life more at your stage of evolutionary development. The delay of your development, which we observe, has been provoked by the influence of the opposing forces. You must realize that there are two opposite forces acting in your world: one force aimed at the Common Weal and Good, and the other force aimed at separation, individualization, egoism, and the boost of the most inferior instincts.

You have to see the work of these two forces behind all the manifestations that are taking place in your world. This will have to do to begin with. You observe all that is happening around you and ask one question only: "What forces benefit from what is happening?"

And if you observe uncontrollable inflation of demands or a tendency towards licentious behavior, you must realize that any kind of attention to such processes — both positive and negative — nurtures them with your Divine Energy.

That is why we give the Teaching on non-violence, because it is useless to struggle against the evil. It starts absorbing your energy and multiplies.

At the same time you must realize that each of you has his own stage of evolutionary development. Each of you has his own degree of transmission of the Divine Energy.

If you are a developed individual, your chakras are open, and you transmit the Divine Energy of a high quality into your world. Therefore, for you, any incorrect use of the energy creates more karma, even a thought of censure concerning the low quality manifestations of the world.

Most people, who read our Messages, still cannot transmit a significant amount of pure energy. The chakras are littered and cannot handle a stronger flow of energy. Your stage of development assumes your active involvement in the processes of the interaction of the opposing forces acting in your world. By your active deeds against the evil and by your standing for the Good, both in your thoughts and in your actions, you facilitate your own development and the opening of your chakras.

Therefore, the Teaching that we are giving on non-violence will be used by individuals standing at different stages of evolution in different ways.

Standing for the principles of the Common Weal and Good requires active deeds from you in the physical plane. For some of you these deeds are connected with real actions in the physical plane in the form of deeds and physical acts, while for other more developed individuals, the work of inner spiritual muscles is required.

I can assure you that at this stage of human evolution very few individuals have a high spiritual level of development. Therefore, your primary mission is to help these individuals maintain Divine patterns.

Sooner or later, from the chaos existing in the world now, we will manage to create the society that will meet the requirements of the Golden Age.

In order for the Golden Age to come as soon as possible and with the least amount of human losses, you need to have a conscious approach to the processes taking place and the understanding of them.

During the cycles of our talks and thanks to your daily reading of our messages in other times, your consciousness is being polished and changed. Those people, who have been reading our messages every day for seven years and longer, are automatically included in the golden reserves of humanity.

Therefore, the whole secret of further successful advancement along the Path of evolution is inherent in our messages and has already been given to you.

It all depends on your aspiration and the motive you are guided by in your life.

**I AM Sanat Kumara. Om.**

# Your task is to save your soul

**June 20, 2014**

I AM Sanat Kumara.

I have come today exactly at the time scheduled by us.

As always I intend to use this Divine opportunity in order to give our Knowledge and understanding of the transformations taking place on the Earth to humanity living on the Earth now.

We have stated in our previous Messages many times that the vibrations of the physical plane of planet Earth are rising. We have told you what you have to do so that your own vibrations and the level of your consciousness correspond to the new reality.

Those of you who have steadily followed our recommendations received an unprecedented leap in your development. Unprecedented opportunities and prospects for inner development are open to you. You are on the top of the wave of the Divine opportunity, and this will allow your soul to continue its evolution at the new level.

You have managed to use the given opportunity! You have managed to seize our helping hand and heeded our advice!

It did not happen to the majority of mankind, however. Most people got into the whirling of energies and are not aware of all the processes taking place.

They are in a situation where the new energies are ousting all karmic blocks from their being, all the blockages of old energies. This resembles a spring cleaning that you do in your home. You shake up old stuff, sweep up the garbage, and chaos and mess swirl around you for a while.

Do not wait for somebody to come and clean up the mess in your house. You are the only person who can put things in order within your being and nobody else.

Therefore, we warned that every one of you who is living on the planet at this transitional time will have to make his choice and will make it.

Now, as with all unattractive general situations on the planet, you have an unprecedented opportunity for your own development.

What was quietly hidden in the depth of your being in old times, centuries ago, has now risen to the surface thanks to the energies of change.

You can notice it in yourselves and observe it literally everywhere.

Is it good or bad? Undoubtedly it is not very good for problem-free living in the physical plane, but it is a great opportunity for the development of your souls.

We have gotten a tremendous Divine dispensation for the transmission of our Messages in advance, ten years before this moment. Our Messages are meant for helping your souls get prepared for the energy leap.

And indeed, many received our help. We only regret that the number of people who have gotten our help and support is not very big.

Even among those people who could get in touch with our Messages thanks to their karma or vibrational level, the percentage of individuals who accurately follow our recommendations is not very high.

You read our Messages and continue your usual way of life. You cannot still believe that simply following our recommendations you will make your living much easier, and you will definitely save your soul.

The lack of faith impedes humankind to take our recommendations seriously. The lack of faith is the stumbling block for many souls.

I will explain to you why you are afraid to believe, why you are so wary about any new teaching and even about old religions.

There is no other sphere of human life where there are so many distortions as in the sphere of faith. This is obvious and realized. In essence, the matter of faith is the most important matter for every human being. If you have faith and you are sincere in your faith, you are already saved.

That is why our opposing forces do everything to compromise every source of Truth in your world and every true Teaching. The most common way is to create many false teachings and sects. In such an abundance of lies not only faith is lost but also hope for a better future.

The next method that our opposing forces use includes lies and slander. All the authentic things are blackened and dragged through the mud. This alienates many sincere seekers of Truth and draws them away from the Divine Path of development.

So, what is offered in turn? You are offered numerous temptations and a great many traps in the physical plane, and when you get into these you are cut off from the evolutionary path of development.

Your Path is the Path of Initiations. You are facing the hardest tests and obstacles on this Path.

Only the most faithful one is capable of overcoming all the traps and temptations of the physical world.

Therefore, do remind yourself of God and the Supreme reality throughout your daily life.

No hour of your life should be lived without God. Only when you are constantly focused on the Supreme reality, do you become invulnerable to the opposing forces and acquire the gift of distinguishing between what is beneficial for the development of your soul and what causes irreparable harm.

I would like to draw your attention to this fact once again: The current period of time is primarily a time to separate those souls who are capable of further evolution from those who are not capable.

Your time provides you with tremendous opportunities for your spiritual growth. You can easily discern on which side everyone is acting. This is due to the fact that politicians, financial dealers, representatives of the governments, and authorities cannot hold fine-looking masks on their faces any longer.

All the masks are thrown off, and it becomes obvious who takes which side.

When you see or know who takes the side of non-divine forces but continue supporting them because of your fear or profit, you factually take the side of these forces.

Therefore, before making any decision in your life, thoroughly weigh all the consequences that it will first bring to your soul.

Your physical body will be left in the earth; your task is to save your soul.

That is why all wise men of all times preferred saving their soul to losing their body.

Think over this Message of mine.

**I AM Sanat Kumara. Om.**

# We are asking you to focus all your strength on sustaining your inner balance

## December 20, 2014

I AM Sanat Kumara.

I have come today with the new Message, an important Message.

You know that now the Earth is going through a very difficult period of its evolution. We can compare this to some sudden changes in your life, for example.

You went to school and the time has come to finish it and to transit into the life of an adult.

You have entered into maturity and it is time to get married.

Every time you experience changes in your lives, you have to adapt to a new way of living and rearrange your life in accordance with that.

This is what is happening on planet Earth now. We have spoken many times about the upcoming changes, we have spoken about the rising of the vibrations, and we have warned that you need to transform yourself, your consciousness and to attune it with the Divine world.

We repeated all that in our Messages many times. You are also aware that only those souls who are attuned to God and stand ready to go along the Supreme Path will be able to continue the evolution on planet Earth.

And now the whole planet is entering the final phase of this process of changes.

For some of you this stage will be a great Divine opportunity to speed up your evolution.

But for some people, on the contrary, this will be a very hard time. By this time each of you has already made his choice between the mortal and the immortal.

You either have committed your lives with the physical plane of the planet or you have chosen the eternal life.

By now this choice has been made by all the souls who are incarnated on planet Earth.

This choice may not reach your external consciousness, but you can indirectly see the choice made by you by the fruits that are manifested in the physical plane.

Look at your life as if from the outside and analyze it. If you have still been unable to submit your life to the Higher Law that exists in this Universe, it inevitably manifests in your life as the desire to acquire the benefits of your civilization at any cost. Sometimes at the neighbor`s expense and in defiance of common sense you seek to take an extra piece, whether it is a sausage, some land on the sea shore, a prestigious post, or some pleasure.

You can be rich or poor, healthy or sick. The whole question is whether you are ready to renounce the high principles of morality and ethics in order to get something for yourself in your world, or whether you are ready to sacrifice much for the sake of the world's wellbeing so that the Earth can continue its evolution and all living creatures can happily live on the planet.

It is so little that a human needs to be happy. You just need to be attuned to the Higher world and to live for the sake of your neighbor.

Many people think that the poor and needy people are closer to God, and where there is wealth there are all the vices and abuses.

No, beloved, it is characteristic of your time that everything is mixed up. There are people who have chosen God both among the rich and the poor, and there are people who are the slaves of their insatiable desires.

Many think that sick people have their diseases because they have torn themselves from God.

No, beloved, there are people who have made completely opposite choices among those who are sick and among those who are healthy.

That is why we are telling you that it is very hard to live in your time. And that is exactly why your time gives great opportunities for the development of some souls and offers the last chance to the others.

It is characteristic of this time that many of you will be enlightened going through great suffering.

Many times we have suggested that you go along the royal road, along the path of changing your consciousness. But most of you have chosen a hard path, the path of hardship and misfortunes, sufferings and losses.

Well, God and the Ascended Masters respect the choice of each of you.

We will be staying beside you no matter what hardship or sufferings fall to your lot in the near future.

You just have to ask for our help, and the help will be given to all who ask and pray. However, you must know that this help will be given to your soul. A great descent of human karma will be taking place in the physical plane.

Unfortunately, there is very little that can be changed.

All your self-sacrifice and self-denial are needed from those of you who are quite aware of the things that are taking place in order to take care of yourself, of your neighbors, and of as many souls as possible in the forthcoming and near future. And sometimes those will be completely unknown people to you.

The situation worsens due to the fact that even very light souls do not have a chance to get sufficient amount of Divine Energy that can allow them to keep their positive mood and joy after getting in touch with the Higher worlds.

Therefore, direct all your power to keep the balance of energies within yourself. Remember that the outer things follow your inner state.

There are many practices and methods that allow sustaining inner peace and harmony. The efforts of those of you who have accrued this special momentum of attainments for the last ten years that we have been giving our Messages will be indispensable.

Each of you becomes as good as gold. You literally can stop any hurricane, any natural calamity, any war or aggression.

All depends on your sustaining the inner balance.

Other people, mass media, and the environment will provoke you and create tension and aggression.

Your task is to transform any negativity into Love and goodness by the flames of your hearts.

We are asking you to focus all your strength and efforts on sustaining your inner balance in the near future.

God help you!

**I AM Sanat Kumara. Om.**

# You can turn around and get back to the Divine Path of development at any point of the path

**December 20, 2015**

I AM Sanat Kumara. I have come again.

It is sad to watch what is happening on Earth at this difficult time.

It could be possible to avoid the worst scenarios.

We are ready to do everything possible and impossible in order to save the biggest possible number of human souls.

However, beloved, now it is your turn. Do you yourselves wish salvation?

Do you have the strength to continue Life?

How it is sometimes difficult to understand what prevents you from returning to the Divine Path.

What prevents you from finding inner confidence in the existence of God and Eternal Life?

Within just a few years, faith in God alone is able to return both the Divine models and the Moral Law into your life.

However, in order to experience the true faith, you have to work hard on yourself. And at least you should follow the recommendations that we have been giving over the past ten years through our Messenger. Is it difficult for you to follow our advice and recommendations?

Why do you prefer to drift down in a muddy stream of surrogates kindly offered to you by the mass media?

Why don't you make any effort to protect yourselves and your children from everything that cripples your souls and restricts your ability and strength to go along the Path of Light?

It is never too late.

You may turn around and get back to the Divine Path of development at any point of the path.

Haven't we told you about it?

Yes, great karma has been created. Yes, it is difficult to break out of the low-grade energies and negative states of your consciousness.

We teach that the confession of the sins and repentance for the committed mistakes can relieve half of the karmic burden, and the other half can be neutralized by the pure energies of prayers.

If the most conscious part of humanity cannot accept Our recommendations and follow Our advice, another path opens up, a harder path, the path of sufferings.

I must tell you that humankind has already stepped over the threshold and is taking its first steps along the path of sufferings.

Many of you complain about your lives, about the lack of joy and love in your lives. However, these are only the first steps along the path of sufferings that you have chosen. So you can imagine what is awaiting you ahead.

We have always showed humanity an easier path. We continue rendering all the necessary help so that at least a small number of souls can choose the path of salvation and follow it. We continue applying our efforts even when the dispensation of the transmission of our Messages is over.

Each of Us has sacrificed the energy of our personal attainments in order to come and give a Message to humanity. Each of Us is doing everything possible and even the impossible. We are applying all the power that the Karmic Board allows.

However, our more subtle energies go past your consciousness because your consciousness is constantly deep in the negative vibrations of the surrounding reality.

That is why we tirelessly remind you of the fact that in order for you to use our help and support, you should do everything possible to maintain your vibrations at the highest possible level.

Unfortunately, it becomes impossible in big cities. Cities are the bastions of those forces that have wrapped humankind and do not give it any chance to follow the evolutionary path.

We lost our battle for cities.

However, those people who live in small settlements are still capable of perceiving Our vibrations and keep their consciousness at quite a high level.

We have done everything possible in order for you to move out of the cities. Modern technologies allow you to have quite comfortable conditions even staying away from the cities.

However, it is impossible to act instead of you in the physical plane.

We have taken all the necessary steps in advance in order to ease your transition and your sufferings. But we cannot do your part of work for you.

Do understand that the time interval is coming when it is possible that you will not be able to get back on the safe evolutionary path.

And this is your choice.

No matter how hard it is to observe your taking steps toward the abyss, We cannot stop you if you decide to jump into it.

I have come today in the hope to bring home to your consciousness this truth that the final chance to avoid the path of sufferings is coming.

This opportunity is still open for the chosen ones.

**I AM Sanat Kumara.**

**Sanat Kumara**

This article is an attempt to present to the World the Image of the Great Wiseman and a Leader of the humanity of the Earth, Sanat Kumara.

**The name Sanat Kumara**

For many centuries the name of Sanat Kumara was known by Wisemen of the East, but it was kept secret from western humanity. In religious traditions of the East, Sanat Kumara appears in different roles; each of them unveils a facet of his Divine Self.

In Hinduism, he is worshiped as one of seven sons of Brahma. They are depicted as young men who kept their purity. Solemn Hindu texts also call Sanat Kumara an "Outstanding Wiseman" who knew Brahman. In Sanskrit, the name of "Sanat Kumara" means "Eternal Youth."

In the supreme God of Zoroastrianism, Ahura Mazda, we recognize Sanat Kumara. The name "Ahura Mazda" means "Wise Lord" or "Lord who is endowed with wisdom." He represents the principle of Goodness, being the protector of humanity and an opponent of the principle of Evil.

In the Old Testament, Sanat Kumara is known as "Eternal God." The prophet Daniel says, "...the Ancient

223

of Days took his seat; his clothing was white as snow, and the hair of his head like pure wool."[10]

In the 20th century, the name of Sanat Kumara became well-known to western humanity. This name was written straightforward in the book *The Secret Doctrine*.[11] It is now known that Helena Petrovna Blavatsky wrote this book with the direct participation of spiritual Beings who had achieved a high level of evolution and now help people to climb the same stairs. That is why this source of information deserves special attention.

In *The Secret Doctrine*, the sacred name is written as one word: "Sanatkumara." Sanatkumara is called Radiant Son of Dawn Manvantara, Dhiani, Dhyan-Chohan, Anupadaka, one of Seven Mind-Born Sons of Brahma, Manu, Son of Fire, Eternal God, the highest Spirit on the ladder of Being, as well as many other titles. Using the analogy of a person, a particular person can play many different roles with many attributes: at the same time he can be a son, a husband, a father; he has a profession, a degree, and he is a member of an organization, so he plays many roles in his life. In the same way, Sanat Kumara has many titles and names depending on the origin, spiritual nature, and form of activity.

---

[10] Daniel 7:9.

[11] Helena P. Blavatsky, *The Secret Doctrine: the Synthesis of Science, Religion, and Philosophy.* London: The Theosophical Publishing Company, 1888. (The book was translated into Russian in 1937 by H.I. Roerich.)

**About *The Secret Doctrine***

To understand who Sanat Kumara is and what His greatness is, we need to become briefly acquainted with some of the basics of ancient Knowledge opened to the Eastern World at the end of the 19th century in *The Secret Doctrine*.

The basis of this writing contains Stanzas from the *Book of Dzyan*. As Helena Blavatsky wrote in the Introduction of *The Secret Doctrine*, "...the chief work — that one from which the Stanzas are given — is not in the possession of European Libraries. The *Book of Dzyan* (or "Dzan") is utterly unknown to our Philologists, or at any rate was never heard of by them under its present name ...but to the students of Occultism, and to every genuine Occultist, this will be of little moment. The main body of the Doctrines given is found scattered throughout hundreds and thousands of Sanskrit MSS., some already translated — disfigured in their interpretations, as usual, — others still awaiting their turn."[12]

Also in the Introduction, the author tells us, "The Secret Doctrine was the universally diffused religion of the

[12] Blavatsky, *The Secret Doctrine,* Volume 1, INTRODUCTORY, page xxvi. Here and further quotations retrieved from *The Secret Doctrine* are given from Theosophical University Press Online Edition, *The Secret Doctrine THE SYNTHESIS OF SCIENCE, RELIGION, AND PHILOSOPHY.* By H. P. Blavatsky. http://holybooks.com/wp-content/uploads/The-Secret-Doctrine-by-H.P.Blavatsky.pdf (The writing of some words and highlighting of text are kept the same as in the original document. (Note: MSS is an abbreviation for manuscripts.)

225

ancient and prehistoric world. Proofs of its diffusion...and presence in every land, together with the teaching of all its great adepts, exist to this day in the secret crypts of libraries belonging to the Occult Fraternity."[13] All of these documents are carefully kept to re-appear in more enlightened times.

*The Secret Doctrine* contains the Stanzas themselves and multiple comments to them. "Extracts are given from the Chinese Tibetan and Sanskrit translations of the original Senzar Commentaries and Glosses on the Book of DZYAN — these being now rendered for the first time into a European language."[14] In addition, the author gives explanations of symbols and definitions in the second part of the book.

"The Stanzas give an abstract formula which can be applied to all evolution: to that of our tiny earth, to that of the chain of planets of which that earth forms one, to the solar Universe to which that chain belongs, and so on, in an ascending scale... The seven Stanzas given in this volume[15] represent the seven terms of this abstract formula. They refer to, and describe the seven great stages of the evolutionary process, which are spoken of in the Purânas[16] as the "Seven Creations," and in the

---

[13] Blavatsky, *The Secret Doctrine*, Vol. 1, INTRODUCTORY, page xxxiv.

[14] Blavatsky, *The Secret Doctrine*, Vol. 1, page 23.

[15] In the 1st Volume of *The Secret Doctrine* seven Stanzas are introduced; in the 2nd Volume, twelve Stanzas.

[16] Purânas are ancient Hindu texts eulogizing various deities, primarily the Divine Trimurti God in Hinduism through Divine stories. Purânas may also be described as a genre of important

Bible as the "Days" of Creation."[17] The Book of Dzyan is more ancient than Indian Vedas, not to mention the Bible.

Any act of creation includes the generation of an idea and then the translation of this idea into action. According to *The Secret Doctrine*, the act of creation of the Universe begins from the Highest Spirit, also named Absolute, absolute Principle, Atman, everlastingly-incognizable Divinity, Parabrahm (of the Hindus), etc., and transforms from an unmanifested condition to a manifested one. "The male-female Potency becomes or expands itself into the manifested Universe," becoming "the manifested WORD or Logos."[18] After that, multiple differentiations and the creation of new "forms" happen, beginning from Divine consciousness and descending to physical matter.

### Dhyan-Chohans

Among those who wake up to an active life on a definite stage of Creation are the so-called firstborn Creatures, Dhyani-Buddhas or Dhyan-Chohans – the Builders of the visible World. These few celestial beings are mediators between the Highest and the

---

Hindu religious texts alongside some Jain and Buddhist religious texts, notably consisting of narratives of the history of the universe from creation to destruction, genealogies of kings, heroes, sages, and demigods, and descriptions of Hindu cosmology, philosophy, and geography (Wikipedia).

[17] Blavatsky, *The Secret Doctrine*, Vol. 1, page 20.

[18] Blavatsky, *The Secret Doctrine*, Vol. 1, page 7.

lowest. "Thus from Spirit, or Cosmic Ideation, comes our consciousness; from Cosmic Substance the several vehicles in which that consciousness is individualized and attains to self — or reflective — consciousness."[19]

Christians know Dhyan-Chohans as Archangels; Hindus call them Rishi-Prajâpati; Jews — Elohims or God's Sons. For all nations they are Planetary Spirits who became Gods to people. The essence of Dhyan-Chohans is opened metaphorically in the comments to Stanza 1: "The AH-HI (Dhyan-Chohans) are the collective hosts of spiritual beings — the Angelic Hosts of Christianity, the Elohim and 'Messengers' of the Jews — who are the vehicle for the manifestation of the Divine or universal thought and will. They are the Intelligent Forces that give to and enact in Nature her 'laws,' while themselves acting according to laws imposed upon them in a similar manner by still higher Powers. However, they are not 'the personifications' of the powers of Nature, as erroneously thought. This hierarchy of spiritual Beings, through which the Universal Mind comes into action, is like an army — a 'Host,' truly — by means of which the fighting power of a nation manifests itself, and which is composed of army corps, divisions, brigades, regiments, and so forth, each with its separate individuality or life, and its limited freedom of action and limited responsibilities; each contained in a larger individuality, to which its own interests are subservient, and each containing lesser individualities in itself."[20] Let us be aware that

---

[19] Blavatsky, *The Secret Doctrine*, Vol. 1, page 16.

[20] Blavatsky, *The Secret Doctrine*, Vol. 1, page 38.

Dhyan-Chohans take a high position of Hierarchy of spiritual Beings. They are "generals" managing their multiple "troops," and at the same time subordinate to "generalissimo." There is a clear hierarchic subordinacy and assignment of duties and responsibility within these spiritual "troops."

In the Stanza IV commentary, the Dhyan-Chohans are called Kumaras, Sons of Fire, the Agnishwatha, and Seven Mystic Sages. "They are — 'The Sons of Fire'— because they are the first Beings (in *The Secret Doctrine* they are called 'Minds'), evolved from Primordial Fire. 'The Lord is a consuming Fire' (Deuteronomy iv. 24)."[21] The Author explains: "Fire is an Æther in its purest form, and hence is not regarded as matter, but it is the unity of an Æther — the second manifested deity — in its universality."[22]

Dhyan-Chohans are also mentioned as Manus (in the comments to Stanza III). Manu is a patron of his special cycle (or Round), "each of the Manus, therefore, being the special god, the creator and fashioner of all that appears during his own respective cycle of being or Manvantara."[23] [24]

---

[21] Blavatsky, *The Secret Doctrine*, Vol. 1, page 87.

[22] Blavatsky, *The Secret* Doctrine, Vol. 1, page 87.

[23] Manvantara literally means "between two Manus." A full period of one Manvantara is 308,448,000 years. Fourteen Manvantatras make one Kalpa, or one day in the life of a creator of the Universe, Brahma.

[24] Blavatsky, *The Secret Doctrine*, Vol. 1, page 63.

**The Kumaras**

The author provides a description of the Kumaras in one of the esoteric texts: *"The Kumâras are the Dhyanis, derived immediately from the supreme Principle, who reappear in the Vaivasvata Manu period,*[25] *for the progress of mankind."*[26]

There are seven Kumaras; four of them are often mentioned in exoteric texts, but three of them are secret. "The Exoteric four are: Sanat-Kumara, Sananda, Sanaka, and Sanatana; and the exoteric three are: Sana, Kapila, and Sanat-sujâta."[27] But, the Author states that these names are just aliases.

Kumaras are present in every religion under different names. The Author mentions seven or ten deities. "Our races have sprung from divine races, by whatever name they are called. Whether we deal with the Indian Rishis or Pitris; with the Chinese Chim-nang and Tchan-gy – their 'divine man' and demi-gods; with the Akkadian Dingir and Mul-lil -- the creative god and the 'Gods of the ghost-world'; with the Egyptian Isis-Osiris and Thot; with the Hebrew Elohim, or again with Manco Capac and his Peruvian progeny — the story varies nowhere. Every nation has either the seven and ten Rishis-Manus and Prajâpatis; the seven and ten Ki-y; or ten and

---

[25] Vaivasvata Manu – is the seventh Manu, Manu of Fifth Root Race.

[26] Blavatsky, *The Secret Doctrine*, Vol. 1, page 456.

[27] Blavatsky, *The Secret Doctrine*, Vol. 1, page 457.

seven *Amshaspends*[28] (six esoterically), ten and seven Chaldean Anedots, ten and seven Sephiroth, etc., etc. One and all have been derived from the primitive Dhyan-Chohans of the Esoteric doctrine, or the 'Builders' of the Stanzas (Book I.)"[29]

### What role did Kumaras play in the development of humanity?

Sons of Fire (Solar Deities) were the ancestors of "the true spiritual SELF in the physical man" (Christ Self, or Highest Manas), while the Pitris (Lunar Deities), are "the fathers of the model, or type of his physical form, made 'in *their* image.' "[30]

The second volume of *The Secret Doctrine* describes the formation of the Root Races of humanity: "The lunar gods (are) ordered to create. The higher gods refuse."

"12. THE GREAT CHOHANS (Lords), CALLED THE LORDS OF THE MOON, OF THE AIRY BODIES (a). 'BRING FORTH MEN, (they were told), MEN OF YOUR NATURE. GIVE THEM (i.e., the Jivas or Monads) THEIR FORMS WITHIN. SHE (Mother Earth or Nature) WILL BUILD COVERINGS WITHOUT (external bodies).'

---

[28] "The Amshaspends are six — if Ormazd, their chief and Logos, is excluded. But in *The Secret Doctrine* he is the seventh and highest, just as Phtah is the seventh Kabir among the Kabiri." (Remark of H.P. Blavatsky, Vol. 2 page 365.)

[29] Blavatsky, *The Secret Doctrine*, Vol. 2, page 366.

[30] Blavatsky, *The Secret Doctrine*, Vol. 1, page 457.

"13. THEY (the Moon-gods) WENT, EACH ON HIS ALLOTTED LAND: SEVEN OF THEM, EACH ON HIS LOT. THE LORDS OF THE FLAME REMAINED BEHIND. THEY WOULD NOT GO, THEY WOULD NOT CREATE."[31]

Among those who "refused to create progeny," the author mentioned Sanat Kumara. "Kumaras who appear on the scene of action by *refusing* — as Sanatkumara and Sananda — to 'create progeny.' Yet they are called the 'creators' of (thinking) man."[32]

The esoteric significance of the Sons of Fire refusing to "create progeny" is explained in the following way: "The 'Rebels' would not create will-less irresponsible men, as the 'obedient' angels did; nor could they endow human beings with only the temporary reflections of their own attributes; for even the latter, belonging to another and a so-much higher plane of consciousness, would leave man still irresponsible, hence interfere with any possibility of a higher progress. No spiritual and psychic evolution is possible on earth — the lowest and most material plane — for one who on that plane, at all events, is inherently perfect and cannot accumulate either merit or demerit. Man remaining the pale shadow of the inert, immutable, and motionless perfection, the one negative and passive attribute of the real *I am that I am*, would

---

[31] Blavatsky. *The Secret Doctrine*, Vol. 2, Stanza III, Pages 75-77. (a) Who are the Lords of the Moon? In India they are called Pitris or "lunar ancestors," but in the Hebrew scrolls it is Jehovah himself who is the "Lord of the Moon."

[32] Blavatsky, *The Secret Doctrine*, Vol. 2, page 584.

have been doomed to pass through life on earth as in a heavy dreamless sleep; hence a failure on this plane."[33]

So Lunar Deities who did not have mind, sent out of themselves creatures like unto themselves, and created their aerial-transparent twins who were future bodily forms of a person. Why is it that Fire Deities "would not want to create" from an objective point of view? Because fire substance is too thin to create future humans' bodies, while the astral matter of Lunar Deities is much closer to the physical plane, even if its density is very different. That is why millions of years were required for the condensation of astral matter to the physical plane matter and for humans to get a bone skeleton and flesh and become the way that we look today.

In the period of Third Root Race (about 18,000,000 years ago), a distinguishing moment for humanity happened: Sons of Fire gave to human forms a "flash" of mind, which is the ability to think. When humanity became physically ready, Fire Gods (Kumaras or Dhyan-Chohans) descended ("fell") into the matter, and in this way they speeded up the evolution of humanity on earth. They not only endowed the biggest part of humanity with mind, but also incarnated in some of the human bodies and gave them knowledge and will. Without this, a person could have never become who he is now.

"27. THE THIRD RACE BECAME THE VAHAN OF THE LORDS OF WISDOM. IT CREATED 'SONS OF WILL AND YOGA,' BY KRIYASAKTI IT CREATED

---

[33] Blavatsky, *The Secret Doctrine*, Vol. 2, page 243.

THEM, THE HOLY FATHERS, ANCESTORS OF THE ARHATS..."[34]

The author comments on this Stanza of the *Book of Dzyan* in this way: "The Third Race had thus created the so-called SONS OF WILL AND YOGA, or the 'ancestors' (the *spiritual* forefathers) of all the subsequent and present Arhats, or Mahatmas... For creation is but the result of will acting on phenomenal matter, the calling forth out of it the primordial divine *Light* and eternal *Life*. They were the 'holy seed-grain' of the future Saviours of Humanity."[35]

"The 'Sons of Wisdom' who incarnated in this Third Race, produced by Kriyasakti a progeny called the 'Sons of Will and Yoga,' etc. They were a conscious production, as a portion of the race was already animated with the Divine spark of spiritual, superior intelligence. It was not a Race, this progeny. It was at first a wondrous Being, called the 'Initiator,' and after him a group of semi-divine and semi-human beings.... they are those in whom are said to have incarnated the highest Dhyanis, 'Munis and Rishis from previous Manvantaras' — *to form the nursery* for future human adepts, on this earth and during the present cycle. These 'Sons of Will and Yoga' born, so to speak, in an immaculate way, remained, it is explained, entirely apart from the rest of mankind. The 'BEING' just referred to, which has to remain nameless, is the *Tree* from which, in subsequent ages, all the great *historically*

---

[34] Blavatsky, *The Secret Doctrine*, Vol. 2, page 19.

[35] Blavatsky, *The Secret Doctrine*, Vol. 2, page 173.

known Sages and Hierophants, such as the Rishi Kapila, Hermes, Enoch, Orpheus, etc., have branched off."[36]

If Dhyan-Chohans had not endowed human forms of the Third Race with Highest Light of Mind (Christ Self or the Highest Manas), how many more hundreds of millions of years would have been needed for a person to become conscious? The animal-person could never have achieved this goal by himself. He would have continued his existence almost unconsciously, like we can see in some of the animals' examples.

After giving such a worthy gift to humanity, the Kumaras did not leave without further help. They reincarnated in Lemurian, Atlantean, and Aryan Races in the roles of Wisemen and Hierophants, and as great Governors and Founders of religions. All Wisemen of ancient times tell us "...of the seven primitive and dual gods who descend from their celestial abode[37] and reign on Earth, teaching mankind Astronomy, Architecture, and all the other sciences that have come down to us. These Beings appear first as 'gods' and Creators; then they merge in nascent man, to finally emerge as 'Divine-Kings and Rulers.' But this fact has been gradually forgotten."[38]

The author points out that "The Aryan nations could trace their descent through the Atlanteans from the more

---

[36] Blavatsky, *The Secret Doctrine*, Vol. 1, page 207.

[37] In the *Purâna* it is identified with Vishnu's or Brahma's Sveta Dwipa of Mount Meru.

[38] Blavatsky, *The Secret Doctrine*, Vol. 2, page 366.

spiritual races of the Lemurians, in whom the 'Sons of Wisdom' had personally incarnated."[39]

"Sons of Wisdom" is another name of the same seven Dhyan-Chohans. In the *Bhagavatgita* they are also called great Rishi. "Let us bear in mind that the Saptarshi (the seven Rishis) are the regents of the seven stars of the Great Bear, therefore, of the same nature as the angels of the planets, or the seven great Planetary Spirits. They were all reborn, all men on earth in various Kalpas and races."[40]

When learning about the role of the Kumaras in the development of humanity, it is impossible not to mention a great error in earthbound minds about their role. In many world religions the act of the Highest Help, which was performed according to the Law of Evolution (The Higher is designated to help the Lower), is considered as the falling of angels "into the darkness of hell." In *The Secret Doctrine*, this act is called the great "self-sacrifice for the good of humanity."

"...the *Secret Doctrine* teaches that the Fire-Devas, the Rudras, and the Kumaras, the 'Virgin-Angels,' (to whom Michael and Gabriel, the Archangels, both belong), the divine 'Rebels' — called by the all-materializing and positive Jews, the Nahash or 'Deprived' — preferred the curse of incarnation and the long cycles of terrestrial existence and rebirths, to seeing the misery (even if unconscious) of the beings (evolved as shadows out of

---

[39] Blavatsky, *The Secret Doctrine*, Vol. 2, page 318.

[40] Blavatsky, *The Secret Doctrine*, Vol. 2, page 318.

their Brethren) through the semi-passive energy of their too *spiritual* Creators. If "man's uses of life should be such as neither to animalize nor to spiritualize, but to *humanize* Self,"[41] before he can do so, he must be born human not angelic. Hence, tradition shows the celestial Yogis offering themselves as voluntary victims in order to redeem Humanity — created god-like and perfect at first — and to endow him with human affections and aspirations. To do this they had to give up their natural status and, descending on our globe, take up their abode on it for the whole cycle of the Mahayuga, thus exchanging their impersonal individualities for individual personalities — the bliss of sidereal existence for the curse of terrestrial life. This voluntary sacrifice of the Fiery Angels, whose nature was *Knowledge* and *Love*, was construed by the esoteric theologies into a statement that shows 'the rebel angels hurled down from heaven into the darkness of Hell' — our Earth."[42]

---

[41] Note from *The Secret Doctrine*, Vol 2, page 246: Explaining the Kabala, Dr. H. Pratt says, "Spirit was to man (to the Jewish Rabbin, rather?) a bodiless, disembodied, or deprived, and degraded being, and hence was termed by the ideograph Nahash 'Deprived'; represented as appearing to and seducing the human race — men through the Woman. ...In the picture from this Nahash, this spirit was represented by a serpent, because from its destitution of bodily members, the Serpent was looked upon as a deprived and depraved and degraded creature" ("New Aspects," p. 235). Symbol for symbol there are those who would prefer that of the serpent — the symbol of wisdom and eternity, deprived of limbs as it is — to the Jod — the poetical ideograph of Jehovah in the Kabala — the god of the male symbol of generation."

[42] Blavatsky, *The Secret Doctrine*, Vol. 2, page 246.

The above mentioned Miraculous Being or "Initiator" created by Dhyan-Chohans from who they appeared ("were separated", or so to say, in an immaculate way) as the "Sons of Will and Yogis," are also called the GREAT SACRIFICE, which the book tells about in a very poetic way:

"He is the 'Initiator,' called the 'GREAT SACRIFICE.' For, sitting at the threshold of LIGHT, he looks into it from within the circle of Darkness, which he will not cross; nor will he quit his post till the last day of this life-cycle. Why does the solitary Watcher remain at his self-chosen post? Why does he sit by the fountain of primeval Wisdom, of which he drinks no longer, as he has naught to learn which he does know — aye, neither on this Earth, nor in its heaven? Because the lonely, sore-footed pilgrims on their way back to their home are never sure to the last moment of not losing their way in this limitless desert of illusion and matter called Earth-Life. Because he would fain show the way to that region of freedom and light, from which he is a voluntary exile himself, to every prisoner who has succeeded in liberating himself from the bonds of flesh and illusion. Because, in short, he has sacrificed himself for the sake of mankind, though but a few Elect may profit by the GREAT SACRIFICE.

"It is under the direct, silent guidance of this MAHA — (great) — GURU that all the other less divine Teachers and instructors of mankind became, from the first awakening of human consciousness, the guides of early Humanity. It is through these "Sons of God" that infant humanity got its first notions of all the arts and sciences, as well as of spiritual knowledge; and it is they

238

who have laid the first foundation-stone of those ancient civilizations that puzzle so sorely our modern generation of students and scholars."[43]

Fortunately, the Great Sons of Wisdom, Dhyan-Chohans, will stay with us until our human evolution will reach the final goal.

Since Dhyan-Chohans are our Grandparents, our spiritual bodies (principles) are identical to their Spiritual Nature. Our task is to go through all the stages of evolution, through multiple cycles of reincarnation according to the Law of Karma, before each of us acquires "individuality, first by natural impulse, and then by self-induced and self-devised efforts (checked by its Karma), thus ascending through all the degrees of intelligence, from the lowest to the highest Manas, from mineral and plant, up to the holiest archangel (Dhyani-Buddha)."[44]

This implies that based on design of God, every person on the path of evolution will become the same as Sanat Kumara at some point!

### Transmitting Knowledge to the World

Throughout time, Sanat Kumara and other Mentors of God have been helping the people of the Earth. We know about the Old Testament's prophet Daniel and about John the Evangelist who beheld the Eternal God.

---

[43] Blavatsky, *The Secret Doctrine*, Vol. 1, page 208.

[44] Blavatsky, *The Secret Doctrine*, Vol. 1, page 17.

We know that outstanding Governors and Founders of religions were conducting Divine Energies to the Earth Divine in one way or another. Recent centuries were not an exception.

The Teachers of humanity send knowledge to this world, which people who achieve a high level of consciousness can perceive. In the 19th century, this person was Helena Petrovna Blavatsky. In the 20th century, a New Teaching of Agni Yoga was received by Elena Ivanovna Roerich while Guy and Edna Ballard, and Mark and Elizabeth Clare Prophet were receiving the messages from Masters of Wisdom. In the 21st century, help to modern humanity comes through Tatyana Nikolaevna Mickushina, who was endowed with a mantle of a Messenger of the Great White Brotherhood.

Since 2005, more than 470 Messages from more the 60 Beings of Light were received by T.N. Mickushina. The Messages tell us about special aspects of our time period and the necessity to change our consciousness.

In our time, the cycles are changing. Humanity has passed the lowest point of materiality and is going Home to the Kingdom of Spirit. The cosmic pendulum has started its movement toward the opposite direction — from spirit going down into matter to its ascension into true reality, and the way will be long. During the next millions of years, a process of decompaction will be taking place, the process of attenuation of matter, and people will be gaining new levels of consciousness, up to the Divine state of consciousness of Dhyan-Chohans.

Masters of Wisdom, beginning with Sanat Kumara, remind us about our Divine origin and call us to wake up to a Higher reality because Divine reality — by its love, wisdom, and beauty — exceeds any of the most wonderful aspects of our physical world.

Sanat Kumara speaks to us through his Messenger, Tatyana Mickushina:

"You are in the physical plane, and you are troubled, first of all, by everything that is happening around you in the physical plane. Yet, we are calling you higher; we are calling you to heavenly peaks, to our world. You will feel yourself in perfect security in our world, under safe control and care.

"You are used to the fact that you come into your cozy physical world from embodiment to embodiment. You feel your unbreakable bond with your physical world. You have created this world. I am telling you that the time has come when you should understand and accept in your consciousness that your world will be transformed. And for those individuals who have not reached a certain level of consciousness the current incarnation may be the last manifestation of their individuality in the physical plane.

"So, think over my words while you still have some time. Accept with your hearts and try to manifest The Great Divine Law in your lives.

"All the perishable that has been created by your imperfect consciousness will cease to exist. Only eternal things will remain: the best manifestations of your Spirit, unselfishness, sacrifice, devotion, the highest manifestation of Love, and many other things will exist with you in the New World. When the old world moves to non-existence, the New World will take its place.

"There will be no place for any human negative manifestations in this world. Only that which is eternal and represents the manifestation of the best human qualities will remain in this world. And these qualities will multiply and grow. All the obsolete will be swept away and destroyed.

"You have nothing to worry and grieve about. Trust the Great Law of the Universe. Nothing will happen to those who believe, to those who love, to those who have hope. Believe me.

"I am with you. All the Ascended Hosts are with you. And we will give our help all the way to everyone who still has the Divine Monad and in whom the Divine essence is manifested.

"None of our people are to fall into non-existence. Everything will be as it is written in the Sacred Books of the past and present.

"God is with you! Do not be afraid of the changes!"[45]

As in *The Secret Doctrine*, the modern Messages also narrate about the Great Deed of Sanat Kumara. In Zarathustra's Message the following is said with great reverence:

"Owing to this Spirit the entire humanity of the Earth was able to continue their evolution. And it is too unjust to forget the great deed of the Spirit of this high individuality. It is too dishonorable to consign to oblivion that Being, owing to whom humanity still continues its evolution.

<...>

"It was many millions of years ago, and the situation on the planet was a good deal like the situation on the planet in your time.

"There was nobody on the whole planet who could sustain the Flame of Life, the Divine fire in his chakras. There was not any being on the planet who could transmit the Divine Energy into the world.

"According to the Law, a world that had withdrawn itself from God was liable for destruction due to its being an unsuccessful civilization.

---

[45] Tatyana Mickushina. Dictation "About the Situation in the World," Sanat Kumara, October 12, 2008. Dictations are available on the websites http://sirius-eng.net (English version) and http://sirius-ru.net (Russian version).

"God had already planned a new lila for planet Earth.

"However, a very high individuality was found who vouched for the planet and for its evolutions.

"And literally in the last moment the decision was made: the evolutions of planet Earth were to continue their existence but only if there was at least one man being in embodiment on the Earth who could sustain the level of the Divine consciousness.

"The first, who assumed the cross of incarnation on the dark planet, was Sanat Kumara. He sacrificed all His attainments in order to come into incarnation and to give the Divine principles of government and understanding of the Divine Law to the evolutions of planet Earth.

"Thanks to this great deed of Spirit millions of life-streams were able to continue the evolution on planet Earth.

<...>

"It is a great grace for the world that Sanat Kumara is continuing His service for the benefit of the evolutions of planet Earth.

"And now, when you know who you are obliged to for the continuation of your evolution, you will not be capable of irresponsibly spending your Divine Energy. For millions of years Sanat Kumara has been crucified on the cross of matter so that your souls could strengthen and assume responsibility upon themselves for the planet and for their own evolution.

"You cannot pretend any longer that you know nothing. You must manifest all your consciousness and be imbued with a sense of reverence before the great sacrifice that Sanat Kumara made for your life-streams."[46]

Now, when the Holy Name of Sanat Kumara and His Great Deed becomes widely known, when the Messages of Sanat Kumara and other Masters of Wisdom are attracted to every person from the pages of the books and computer desktops, then humanity cannot just keep being bound up in the interests of just the physical plane.

A goal and a sense of purpose in peoples' lives are to establish and maintain a connection with the Higher Worlds in their consciousness. When a sufficient number of people are able to go up to the Highest Worlds in their consciousness, all the godlike changes will begin happening in the world. Just by the power of changing our consciousness, we will be able to reform the physical world and carry out our evolutionary mission.

**E.Ilina**

---

[46] Tatyana Mickushina. Dictation "You must be imbued with a sense of reverence about a great sacrifice that Sanat Kumara made for your life-streams," Zarathustra, December 27, 2012. Dictations are available on the websites http://sirius-eng.net (English version) and http://sirius-ru.net (Russian version).

# About the author

Tatyana Nicholaevna Mickushina was born in the south of western Siberia in the town of Omsk. During all of her life, she has been praying and asking God to grant her an opportunity to work for Him.

In 2004, Tatyana N. Mickushina was granted a Messenger's Mantle of the Great White Brotherhood and received an opportunity to bring the Words of the Masters to people. Since 2005, at certain periods of time, she receives messages from the Ascended Masters in a special way. With the help of many people, the messages have been translated into English and many other languages so that more people can become familiar with them.

"The only thing the Ascended Masters want is to spread their Teaching throughout the world.

The Masters give their messages with the feeling of great Love. Love has no limits.

There are no boundaries between the hearts of people living in different countries; there are no boundaries between the worlds. The boundaries exist only in the consciousness of people.

The Masters appeal through me to every person living on planet Earth.

I wish you success on the spiritual Path!"

**Light and Love! Tatyana Mickushina**

**Author page of T. N. Mickushina on Amazon:**
amazon.com/author/tatyana_mickushina

# WORDS OF WISDOM SERIES

The "Words of Wisdom" series of books was created based on the Ascended Masters' Messages that have been given through T.N. Mickushina. Since 2005, she has received over 450 Messages from more than 50 Beings of Light. You can find the Dictations on the website "Sirius" sirius-eng.net (English version) and sirius-ru.net or sirius-net.org (Russian version).

The Ascended Masters have been communicating with mankind for thousands of years. Since ancient times, the Masters of Shambala were known in the East. In different teachings, people call them by different names: the Teachers of Humanity, the Ascended Masters, the Masters of Wisdom or the Great White Brotherhood.

These Teachers have reached the next evolutionary step in their development and continue their development in the Higher planes. These Higher Beings consider it Their duty to help humanity in the development of their consciousness.

The method which the Ascended Masters have chosen to communicate with humanity is the transmission of the Messages (Dictations) that are written by the Messenger who can use a special method to provide the perception of the Messages from the higher, etheric octaves of Light.

The first Dictation from Sanat Kumara on March 4, 2005, gave us the following message:

"I AM Sanat Kumara and I have come today to inform the world about a new opportunity and a new dispensation which the Heavens have decided to free through our new Russian Messenger Tatyana.

This turn of events will be unexpected for many of you. Many of you will experience contradictory feelings while reading this message.

However, we do not want to force anybody to believe or not to believe the things to be told. Our task is to give you this knowledge. Its acceptance is a matter of your own free will.

Times have changed and the New Age has come. The worlds have converged. Things which seemed to be an impossible dream a few years ago, even last year, are starting to become real now. We are getting an opportunity to speak through many of you and we are using this opportunity."

Each of the Masters of Wisdom strives to give us what they consider most vital at the present moment of transition. Every message contains the energies of different Masters who give those messages. The Masters speak about the current historical moment on planet Earth. They tell us about energy and vibrations, about the illusion of this world and about the Divine Reality, about the Higher Self of a human and about his lower bodies. They give us concrete recommendations on exactly how to change our own consciousness and continue on the evolutionary Path.

It is recommended that you prepare yourself for reading every message very carefully.

**Masters of Wisdom**

# SANAT KUMARA

**Dictations through the Messenger
Tatyana Nicholaevna Mickushina
(from 2005 through 2015)**

Tatyana N. Mickushina

**Websites:**

http://sirius-eng.net (English version)
http://sirius-ru.net (Russian version)

Books by T.N.Mickushina on amazon.com:
amazon.com/author/tatyana_mickushina

CPSIA information can be obtained
at www.ICGtesting.com
Printed in the USA
FSHW020846031119
63697FS